For

**William Hynes, Julia Campbell Hynes,
Ursula Warren Whelan and George Whelan**

**Dedicated to my mother
Bernadette Whelan Warner
1951-2008**
Who loved history too!

Introduction by Mayor Marie Corr

FROM 1914-1918, two hundred thousand Irishmen from all religions and backgrounds went to war in Europe and beyond. Tens of thousands of them did not return home. Those who did were not only mentally and physically scarred, but they were often ostracised by their fellow Irishmen for their perceived disloyalty.

Although their skills and expertise were needed and utilised in the subsequent Irish War of Independence, the narrative of ex-British soldiers in the Irish Army has largely been ignored in Irish history.

The recent visit of Queen Elizabeth II to the National War Memorial Gardens at Islandbridge in Dublin, where she laid a wreath in honour of the Irishmen who fought in World War I, went some way to bringing their stories to public consciousness. This book details the immense challenges they faced, and the massive sacrifices and contribution they made for the sake of Ireland's freedom.

It is vitally important to acknowledge that amongst all those who fought for Irish Independence were British trained Irishmen who helped revolutionise the Irish Army and they also fought and died for the promise and ideals of Ireland.

South Dublin County Council is delighted to publish this book as a mark of our respect.

Mayor of South Dublin County

ii

Contents

Acknowledgements

A project such as the research for this book would not be and never is possible without the impact and support of many different people at different levels and in different aspects.

I would like to thank the staff of the History Department of NUI, Maynooth, in particular Professor Vincent Comerford, Professor Jacqueline Hill, Professor Ray Gillespie and Dr Ian Speller. I would like to acknowledge the cooperation of Penny Woods and the staff of the Russell Library, the staff of the National Library of Ireland, Commandant Victor Laing, Captain McEóin and Alan Manning in the Military Archives of Ireland, the staff of the National Archives of Ireland, Trinity College Dublin, University College Dublin Archives and the Staff of Wicklow County Council Libraries in Bray, the staff of the National Museum of Ireland, especially Lar Joye, Glen Thompson and Siobhan Pierce of the 'Soldiers and Chiefs' exhibition at Collins Barracks, Dublin, Dr. Michael Kennedy of the Royal Irish Academy and the National Archives, the Military History Society of Ireland, Military Heritage of Ireland Trust, British National Archives, Reggie Darling and the Curragh History Society, Schull Books, Ballydehob, Karl Murphy, grandson of General WRE Murphy, Margaret Stewart, granddaughter of Henry Stewart.

I would also like to acknowledge the Irish Air Corps, its Photographic Section and Museum. Private Ronnie Daly of the Irish Defence Forces who is an avid researcher and collector of this period and a very interesting man, the Irish Defence Forces Library and Communications Centre in the Curragh camp, in particular Corporal Terry O'Reilly. From the Irish Army – Private Peter McGuinness 27th Battalion, Signalman Paul O'Connor (OC), Corporal Joe Farrelly both 2 Field CIS, Lt Col Brendan O'Shea and Coy Quartermaster Sergeant Chalkie White - both Collins Barracks, Cork and the military museum there, Mr Tony (A.T.) Kearns a long time friend of mine and historian of the Irish Air Corps and Mr Paddy Cummins - Waterford.

I would like to acknowledge also the support of my colleagues and friends in the Irish Defence Forces: my great friend Mr Jarlath Conerney, secretary of the Royal Aeronautical Society and Air Corps Apprentice School, Maj General Ralph James, Deputy Chief of Staff, Brig Gen Paul Fry, GOC Irish Air Corps, Lt Colonel John Moloney, Officer Commanding No. 4 Support Wing, Lt Fabio Scalici, Flight Sergeant Jim Perkins, Lt Colonel John Kirk (ret), Corporal Joey Brosnan, Airman Ciaran Ready, Corporal Paul Carroll, Corporal Pat O'Leary, Airman Paddy Carpenter, Corporal Paddy Gorman, Airman Robbie Duff, Airman Martin Kelly, Airman Willie Lynch, FQMS Tommy Nolan (ret), Sergeant Jimmy Hayles and his father Jim senior (PDF ret), Sergeant Wayne Withero, Commandant Chris McQuaid (ret), Sergeant Charlie Callinan (ret), Flight Sergeant Johnny McEvoy (ret), Sergeant Major Francie O'Brien (ret), Sergeant Shay Singleton, Sergeant Steve Yeats, Sergeant Steve Phelan, Sergeant Tony Farrell, Sergeant Wayne FitzGerald, Sergeant Jack Kilbride (ret), Airman Terry Murray, Airman Martin Gavigan, Airman Niall Boland, Sergeant Ray Hennessy, Airman Pete Cummins, Corporal Tony Flanagan (ret), Corporal John Beirne, Flight Sergeant Pat Casey, Airman Joe O'Hanlon, Corporal Jacko Lane, members of the Roger Casement branch, O.N.E.

Also Airman Stephen O'Gorman, Sergeant Dave Nagle, Airman Billy Galligan and Wesley Bourke from Defence Forces Press Office and Sergeant Paul Walsh, Flight Sergeant Mathew McNamara and all the guys in the Air Corps computer section. A special thank you to Corporal Mark Whelan and Corporal Declan Redmond for all your help with the books and especially the good times over the years, not least since February 12th 1990.

A very big thank you to Kieran Swords, Síle Coleman, Colette Carpenter and South Dublin County Council Libraries and their Local Studies section for seeing the importance of this history and for publishing it. Thanks to Dr Rosaleen Dwyer, Heritage Officer for South Dublin County for your friendship and support and a very special thank you to Colette Allen for your patience in the editing of this book.

I would also like to thank my father-in-law, Mr Eddie Power for his help with reading drafts, my sister, Tracey Pujalis for her help with the typing in the early days, my family including my wife Niamh and children, Mikey and Emily and my Great Uncle Mr Sean Campbell, who passed away in April 2008. He was a former member of the Irish and British Armies and a veteran of the famous Eighth Army of North Africa and Italy during World War II, my father, Michael and last but not least my mother, Bernadette Whelan-Warner, who died in November, 2008, without seeing the final product. She loved history too and anticipated this book even more than me.

Abbreviations

Bureau of Military History	BMH
Dublin Metropolitan Police	DMP
General Head Quarters	GHQ
Irish Air Corps	IAC
Irish Republican Army	IRA
Irish Volunteers	IV
Military Archives of Ireland	MAI
Mulcahy Papers	MP
National Archives of Ireland	NAI
National Library of Ireland	NLI
Royal Irish Constabulary	RIC
Trinity College Dublin	TCD
University College Dublin Archives	UCDA
House of Commons Papers	HC

Terms Used in Text

The Government forces during the Irish Civil War were commonly referred to as the Free State Army, National Army, pro-Treaty forces or the Regulars.

Those opposed to the government were commonly referred to as the IRA, Irish Volunteers (post 1922), anti-Treaty forces, Republicans or Irregulars.

The War of Independence also referred to as the Anglo-Irish War and the Tan War constituted part of this conflict.

Author's Introduction

> **Forgetting . . . is a crucial factor in the creation of a nation**
> Ernest Renen

THE great blood letting of World War I and of Ireland's struggle from 1914-1923 has reached the point in history and collective memory, where although modern Irish politics and society directly reflects those turbulent times, it is relatively forgotten.

To some it has passed into that realm of distant history and legend and myth. The events have indeed passed out of living memory but that does not mean it should be dismissed as being part of that distant past were it can be easily thought of as having no real or general importance. Growing up in Ireland in the 1970s and 80s the national schools I attended had their own iconic symbolism connecting the students to the events of 1916. However in the late eighties I felt there was no real link. It seemed like events of a distant past long ago but maybe this was the way a young boy saw things. If one reflects on the distance in time then it is easy to see that the period in question is very close indeed. For instance, it is only two generations since the birth of my grandfather William Hynes in Chatham Row near Stephens Green in the Dublin of January 1916. His mother would have had to constantly protect him and the rest of her family during the heavy fighting in that area during Easter week. Many civilians died during the period, including children.

His future wife Julia Campbell, the daughter of an Irish born British soldier and WWI veteran, was born in Dublin in 1923 at the time of the Irish Civil War. On my father's side my grandfather George Whelan was born in 1919, the year the troops began to return from the Great War. His future wife Ursula Warren was born in India in 1923, the daughter of an English born WWI veteran.

Although the four have since passed on I have great memories of them and I regret that I was not old enough or interested enough at the time to sit down and ask them about their lives. They were born during the turbulent and historic days discussed in this book. They are my most important and direct link with the past and those events. If my grandparents were alive today they would remember stories of it and pass on their memories and those of their parents. The ninety-year period means a gap of only two or three generations, if you count my children. This is not a long time at all. This is one of the main reasons why I am interested in this period.

People's lives were by no means easy and survival was a tough business. People had diverse backgrounds and reasons for taking their place on either side of the political divide or in the British army or IRA. To understand the conflicts and the period it is important to try to get a grasp of all the levels of society and its different factions and its turning points. One such faction that I believe has not been thoroughly examined is those ex-British soldiers, many of whom were originally Irish Volunteers who later joined the IRA and National Army during the Irish War of Independence and Civil War. How was it that Irishmen who fought in the British forces and who were labelled as traitors, were able to later join the IRA and national army and help bring independence and sovereignty to Ireland? Why are they virtually left out of the Irish historical narrative?

How was it possible that those who had fought for what was said to be an imperial form of independence then joined the conflict endeavouring to achieve full independence from that imperial system in the form of the fight for Ireland's freedom? Their experience meant that these soldiers were able to influence and inspire their comrades to become better soldiers and to carry out their missions professionally. They had fought in the misery of the trenches on the Western front; they had fought in the Middle East, the Balkans and Africa, on the sea and in the air. In reality they fought to survive, they fought for their friends, their families and they fought for the freedom of small nations, ultimately their own. Irish soldiers fought for Ireland in the Great War, the Irish War of Independence and the Irish Civil War. This is the message I hope to bring with this book.

Michael J. Whelan, M.A.

Foreword

THIS long-overdue book deals with an aspect of modern Irish history previously (conveniently?) hidden from Irish public view. Finally an author has firmly grasped this uniquely Irish and enigmatic nettle and produced a well written and detailed study, which speaks volumes about the author's dedication, resourcefulness and integrity. He has produced a clear and readable volume covering this key period in Ireland's recent history. I feel strongly that the reader will, like me, find it both captivating and enthralling.

It is a fascinating and educational production, spanning the key pre-World War I era with all of its promises, the 1916 Rising with its controversy leading into the War of Independence and the final divisive, decisive Civil War conclusion. However, the key topic which makes this book captivating and unique is its focus upon the part played in these three phases of Irish fighting history by former British Army personnel drawn from across that Army's ranks of Officers, NCO's and Men.

The IRA used British Army weapons handling expertise gleaned from its former members in its fight against that very Army on Irish ground. They continued to use this expertise when fighting against the National Army in the Civil War, as did the National Army, the forefathers of today's Oglaigh na h-Éireann, the Permanent Defence Force. For this training expertise to come from the former 'enemy' Army yet feed itself into both sides of the civil war is of note in itself but when the reader remembers that the source of this training was at one time the common enemy of both sides who fought the civil war, its impact and import is even more remarkable.

The National Army benefited from this source of trained ex-British Forces personnel in many Corps' and Services and the fledgling Air Service benefited from the Royal Flying Corps/Air Force in being provided with no less than four Commanding Officers from their ranks. The first was its first OC Air Service Major General

MacSweeney; also to command was Colonel Charles F. Russell, who in turn, handed over to Colonel James Fitzmaurice. Colonel 'Bill' Delamere commanded the Air Corps in the dark days of the early 1940's before finishing an illustrious career in Aer Lingus.

I can recommend this book to students of history with an interest in all aspects of modern 20th Century insurgency and military counter-insurgency operations, but it will be especially recommended to those with an interest in recent modern Irish history.

Brigadier General Paul Fry,
General Officer Commanding at Irish Air Corps.

> **I joined the British Army because she stood between Ireland and an enemy common to our civilization and I would not have her say that she defended us while we did nothing at home but pass resolutions.**
>
> Francis Ledwidge, *Irish poet killed in action WWI*

Preface

One can imagine the sequence of events —

A young man, he could be living in any part of Ireland but he was reared on the age-old stories and histories of Ireland's long struggle with its English oppressor. With this as part of his makeup he joins the Fianna or the Irish Citizen Army or indeed the Irish Volunteers of 1913; he is already involved in the acquisition of arms and is a trusted and militarised soldier of Ireland. In 1914 he sees the political landscape changing, although he does not know exactly what is happening he realises that Ireland has an opportunity for independence. The young man decides to join the British army to help Belgium and other small nations to achieve freedom, defeat Germany's tyranny and do something great for ol' Ireland. He may help Ireland achieve freedom and maybe even become a hero for his country. Besides, the family could do with the money!

The young man attends one of the many recruiting rallies held by the local councils and the army, and convinced of the noble calling and promises of John Redmond's Parliamentary Party that this will bring Irish national aspirations closer, he joins an infantry company which will soon become part of the 29th Division. Many others later joined the newly formed 10th Irish Division. The Division will be made up of Catholics and Protestants from North and South. Many are from the Volunteers and he knows them well, others are from the Loyalist community and many from the Ulster Volunteers. Soon after this the recruits are posted to training grounds in Dublin and from there some go to England for specialist instruction.

By 1915 the young soldier of the 29th Division and hundreds of his comrades from Dublin, Cork, Galway, Wexford, Belfast and many other places in Ireland and Britain find themselves aboard a merchant vessel, a converted collier named the River Clyde, on the approach to 'V' Beach at Suvla Bay as part of the allied assault on the Turkish positions on the Gallipoli Peninsula in the Dardanelles. All the heroic gestures, the idealism, the love of Ireland and his conscience battling over what is the right thing to do, all the flag waving and back slapping as he boarded the train at the start of his long journey to the place where he finds himself now, none of this has prepared him for what he is about to experience.

This British soldier, this young soldier of Ireland moves slowly along in the sluggish procession from the darkness in the bowels of the ships cargo area, one man behind the other looking dead ahead, all weighed down with weapons and backpacks and kit. He catches glimpses of the brightest lights flickering and jumping from metal walls to metal bulkheads to the absorbed faces of innocence as the ship swayed. He wonders what it is like outside in the fresh air and where exactly he is and how funny it is that he finds himself somewhere half way round the world near Greece on a job for Ireland when he had never even left his home town before! The ship comes to an abrupt stop and the sense of urgency is intensified. Now the soldier can hear orders and commands being barked at the human cargo as it lines out in front him. The procession begins to move a little faster along the narrow walkways and up the metal stairways toward the surface decks of the ship, to the light, always upwards toward the light. He longs to be outside in the light. Ahead of him as he approaches the forward end of the ship's interior are two great beams of light, like two massive headlamps moving toward each other and towards the approaching cargo. He finds it hard to focus his eyes upon the lights and notices that the human procession is having the same difficulties as it passes into them in separate lines but there is something else. He hears an intermittent metallic sound like dozens of small hammers impacting on the bulkhead at high speed, sometimes singularly but mostly in long clusters of sound. The pace quickens towards the beams of light and as the men up front pass through them the soldier thinks that they now resemble portals transporting the human cargo out of his vision to somewhere he does not know yet, but soon will. The pace quickens to almost a forced march in the confined space and as the shouting becomes intense and the soldier approaches the portal on the right he is unceremoniously shoved through by one of the hunkering and barking cluster of men in uniform who are crowded on either side of the light. The metallic impacting sound is almost unbearable and he is blinded as he passes through the portal disorientated.

What this young man from Ireland, this soldier, sees before him now, takes his breath away. He stops for a moment to take stock of the images with which he is confronted. Fear and panic suddenly grip him, he is pushed down a wooden gangway from the portal, a large gaping hole cut in the side of the ship to allow the mass exit of troops, down towards a group of barges and smaller boats, which are tethered together from the front of the Clyde towards the beach. From the beginning of each portal on both sides of the ship, which descend from about forty feet down to the plank covered boats, the gangways form a kind of improvised pier upon which dozens of men are trying to cross onto the boats, sand and safety. The soldier trips over a man lying half on and half off the gangway, as he falls and tries to recover himself the metallic impacting noise can be heard but closer now as if he can almost feel it. At the same time, almost as if movement around him is progressing in fractions he notices sparks on the side of the ship. As the sparks arch past the soldiers position again, suddenly the man directly behind him yells and falls from the gangway into the water far below. In shock the young soldier looks forward, realising that he is under fire and absorbs every minute detail of the carnage before him as it unfolds.

Beyond the beach are high bluffs and defences where he sees groups of what look like men directing fire towards the ships dispensing their cargo. To the right of the beach and atop the bluffs stands a block fortification, massive in its structure and resembling a curtain wall not unlike that of a medieval castle. From this fortification murderous fire is poured down onto the beach by Turkish machinegun nests and riflemen. This fire is joining together in a combined repetitive sheet of deadly lead, encasing the beach and the ships and the sea and all the soldiers negotiating their way from the bowels of the Clyde to the base of the beach wall.

Hundreds of men are running, drowning, spinning, crawling and dying, being cut to shreds. Thousands of short white spouts rise from the water or shoot out from its surface towards the beach, some big and some bigger as an enemy bullet strikes it for every splash all around the vessels, which resemble castles of clogged corrals tethered to the beach as men move forward to be slaughtered. The zipping noise of bullets splits the air thousands and thousands of times over and over again. Soldiers manning machineguns and rifles return fire from the forward edge of the battle area and the forward end of the Clyde but they in turn are raked by accurate and deadly fire from the Turkish defences. The boats are filling with casualties, blood is spattered all over and pooling around the decks, rolling over the edge and down the sides of the massive metal hulk to the sea below, the sea, the encompassing sea. The blue and white water has become red as it washes in its new deliveries of human driftwood, being piled high at the waters edge. Men begin to take cover behind this human barricade; their dead comrades will stop bullets that are meant for them. There will be time to worry about them later, time to absorb the unimaginable. The fortified walls and bluffs are being pounded by shells from the naval ships at sea, keeping the Turks' heads down so the men can move towards cover and into the fight but hundreds are being destroyed in such a small space and such a short time. Metal against flesh and guts. Men from the gangway are standing in bunches trying to get onto the boats to cross onto the beach, they are panicked and many seem to falter and spin as bullets rip through their bodies, lines and lines of men spinning and falling. There are ships in the distance, to the left and to the right of the Clyde; the water is still and reflecting a beautiful clear blue sky just beyond them. The glint of the sun upon the surface of the water blurs the soldier's vision of the seabed again and again but he can see the water turning red. Bodies of the men with whom he had been climbing through the darkness of the ship just moments before, are broken together in the dozens in the water and along the shoreline and across the boats and beach. Men are falling all around him and among the chaos and noise, he knows he must get off the gangway or he will die. He cannot go back through the portal; men are still streaming through and becoming casualties, choking the gangway and boats making them easy targets. The soldier holds his breath and runs pushing past the men in the front, across the bodies of men in the boats, some screaming his name and crying for help. Finally he reaches the sand of the beach as large chunks of the wooden boat near to where he is hiding are torn off and thrown through the air by Turkish machinegun fire from the heights above. The sand is red and littered with bodies and cowering soldiers, his friends. He is lost in the horror of it all, the images he is witnessing being seared into his mind. Someone kicks him, yelling 'if your not feckin' dead yet then get your arse off this beach, get to cover by the bluffs and start fightin' back'

In shock the soldier picks himself up and runs almost a hundred yards down the beach over the bodies of his comrades and through the withering fire of enemy soldiers who are trying to kill him. Bullets impact in the sand all around him, pierce his clothing and equipment as he reaches cover and waits for a moment, until his heavy breathing subsides and he can hear his body. Has he been hit? No, he's ok. But he sees from the faces of those men lying everywhere around him that most of those who landed at the same time as him have been hit. He has survived the first part and must somehow fight and survive the rest. He has survived the landing on the Gallipoli Peninsula. He is a soldier of Ireland and has come through his baptism of fire. What will his family think? What will the people back home in Ireland think of his friends and him who are fighting and dying for the promise of Ireland in an English army?

A year later and because of the constant attrition on the soldiers, the young man finds himself fighting with the 16th Irish Division on the Somme. He is not so young looking. Now he is a veteran of many battles. He has seen many friends injured and killed. He is a survivor. He spends his days trying to survive without going crazy in the trenches. It is July 1916 and he is no longer a hero of Ireland but considered a traitor and distrusted by the hierarchy of the British army. The new heroes of Ireland have risen up in insurrection in Dublin and elsewhere in the country proclaiming a Republic. After the Easter Rebellion in April and the subsequent execution of its leaders public opinion had turned against British soldiers and those Irishmen who were serving within its ranks on the promise of Home Rule.

Recruitment in Ireland slowed to a trickle but many thousands of Irishmen were still fighting in the war. After surviving four years of constant combat our soldier is quite a seasoned veteran. In 1919 he returns to Ireland with thousands of demobbed soldiers but not to a hero's welcome like other victorious troops in other countries. The goal posts had moved, no longer is the dream of Home Rule but of a Republic. Ex-soldiers are not wanted, the veterans are an embarrassment and seen as pro-English pawns. They cannot get work, are openly abused and are close to the poverty line. The homecoming and land fit for heroes does not apply to him. Instead the peaceful life and existence that he has promised God he would lead if he managed to survive the war, and which he had been promised and fought for, was about to be shattered.

The Anglo-Irish War commenced and so our soldier joins the local IRA not far from where he had attended the British Army recruiting rally in 1914. Maybe he was idealistic and believed in the Republic or maybe he just needed a role and somewhere to fit in. Whatever the reason the soldier offers his skills and begins training the Volunteers for the fight against the British, his former comrades. Although not trusted greatly in the beginning he soon gains the respect of the movement and goes on active combat missions and helps to professionalise the IRA. He is now a defender of the Republic fighting to remove the British army from Ireland, fighting against soldiers he had fought alongside in Gallipoli and in Europe not long previously. At the end of this war he will join the new Irish National Army and fight against his Republican comrades during the Civil War for a Free State and will train that force too.

This is not an imagined tale it happened to thousands of individuals like the young soldier. These men went from being volunteers and soldiers for Irish freedom to soldiers of the Empire, soldiers of the Irish Republic and soldiers of the Irish Free State. Always it was for Ireland.

> **What it is to me to be called a British soldier while my own country has no place among the nations but the place of Cinderella.**
>
> Francis Ledwidge, *Irish poet killed WWI*

Chapter I

IDEOLOGIES

Background to the Nationalist Origins of the Irish Army 1913-1924

'The spirit of the times during the period of Ireland's revolution held life cheap. 10 million had died in the First World War and the quasi-religious fervour of 1916 still fired the more extreme Republicans. Many young men, imbued with exalted patriotism and having a role for the first time in their mundane lives, welcomed the call to arms'

Edward Purdon[1]

THE evolution of the Irish Free State Army from its foundation as the Irish Volunteers of 1913, through the War of Independence and the Irish Civil War relied greatly on the inclusion of ex-British servicemen. If the army couldn't survive, neither could the State and although the Irish Army as we know it today is not a conventional fighting force one might forget that it is an extremely viable asset wherever it serves throughout the world and at home in Ireland. Because of its success as a major contributor to many United Nations military missions and other peace support missions over the last half-century one might also forget that its foundation belongs in conflict, as does its early evolution.

---

[1] Edward Purdon, *The Civil War 1922-23* (Dublin, 2000), p.15

1

Many constraints and tests are placed on the fledgling military force of an emerging nation and Ireland's was no different. From its beginnings among Volunteers in 1913 it became a functionary tool for the Nationalist's ideals of fighting for an independent Ireland. This tool was then divided between those who supported the Treaty and those who were discontented with it. The purpose of the Volunteers became blurred. Both sides in the ensuing Civil War assumed sole authority and responsibility for what they saw as what the people of the new State desired.

Home Rule had been the key issue that dominated political debate in both Ireland and the United Kingdom since Gladstone's introduction of the First Home Rule Bill of 1886. The Second Home Rule Bill, which was brought forward in 1903 actually passed in the House of Commons but was vetoed by the House of Lords. The Third Home Rule Bill, introduced in April 1912 sparked off a crisis in Ireland where the majority Nationalist population had high hopes of autonomy, and the Unionists in Ulster were opposed to any such notion.

On 28 September 1912, 250,000 Unionists gathered at Belfast's City Hall to sign a "Solemn League and Covenant" pledging to resist Home Rule, some signing in their own blood. By January, 1913, they had formed the nucleus of the military organisation known as the Ulster Volunteer Force (UVF), which was organised to add weight to their threats of resistance to Home Rule, by use of arms if necessary. They would fight against the crown and its forces in order to stay British and were secretly aided by elements within the Conservative Party.

The Nationalist elements within Irish society were alarmed at this development, so much so that the Irish Volunteers *(Óglaigh na hÉireann)* was formed at a huge public meeting held at the Rotunda Rink in Dublin on 25 November of the same year.

At the Rotunda Rink meeting Professor Eoin McNeill spoke to the crowds saying:

> '*We are meeting in public in order to proceed at once to enrolment and organisation of a national force of volunteers. We believe that the national instinct of the people and their reasoned opinion has been steadily forming itself for some time past in favour of the undertaking. All that is now needed is to create a suitable opportunity, to make a beginning and from a public meeting of the most unrestricted and representative kind, in the capital of the country, invite all able- bodied men of Ireland to form themselves into a united and disciplined body of freemen prepared to secure and maintain the rights and liberties common to all the people of Ireland.*'[2]

Eight thousand people from a wide cross section of the community attended this meeting.

The aims of the Irish Volunteers were:

1. To secure and maintain the rights and liberties common to all the people of Ireland.

2. To train for this end, discipline, arm and equip a body of Irish Volunteers.

3. To unite for this purpose all Irishmen without distinction of creed, class or politics.

Their mission was to safeguard the granting of Home Rule in Ireland. From the beginning this movement included, in a clandestine manner, members of the shadowy Irish Republican Brotherhood (IRB) a secret oath-bound society dedicated to the formalising of the Independent Irish Republic, by force of arms if necessary.

---

[2] G White & B O'Shea *The Irish Volunteer Soldier 1913-23* pp 9-12

The IRB leadership saw the Volunteers as the ideal vehicle by which they could manifest their aims. Before long several members of this organisation had infiltrated their way into prominent leading positions within the volunteer movement. This would later prove to be a critical manoeuvre by the IRB. Within six months the Volunteers membership had risen to 75,000, with units formed in most parts of the country.

With the participation of the Irish Parliamentary Party there was another influx of volunteers, which brought the membership to over 160,000. With the outbreak of the First World War, the organisation was to feel the effects of Britain's rule, as was Ireland. In September 1914 King George V signed the Third Home Rule Bill and placed it on the statute book to be implemented twelve months later, or whenever the war ended. These events were to affect people in Ireland in different ways, questioning their loyalties and politics. Some found themselves in unique and even compromised positions.

In 1914, Joseph Patrick Kennedy, born in Dublin in 1894 and educated at the Presentation College, Glasthule, La Sainte Union, des Sacres Convent in Bath, Somerset and later the Jesuit College at Stony Hurst in Lancashire and Trinity College Dublin, was a Catholic shipyard pupil under the tutelage of the Shipbuilding and Engineering Works at Harland and Wolff Ltd. in Belfast. He had acknowledged the political climate in Ulster during this period, especially towards Catholics, and against the wishes of his father found himself training the Irish Volunteers there to oppose the UVF. He was one of those young men who found themselves polarised by political events, but what is interesting is that Joseph and his brothers would later make a family pact with each other, joining the British forces to fight in the war and who so ever should survive would look after the interests of the deceased brothers' families. Joseph joined the Royal Air Force in early 1918 serving in France and like his brothers survived the war.[3] Joseph

---

[3]Material on Joseph P. Kennedy taken from his unpublished memoirs and received from his grandson Michael Kennedy PhD to whom I am extremely grateful. Details with author.

joined the forces quite late and would have known of the animosity towards Irishmen enlisting and would have known also of the carnage and depletion of the youth of countries involved in the war after almost four years.

John Redmond the leader of the Irish Parliamentary Party began to organise and plea for the members of the volunteer movement to enlist in the British Army so as to help bring an end to war in Europe. The hope was that this would bring Home Rule sooner rather than later. The response was overwhelming but eventually split the nationalist movement, which by this time had reached 182,000 members. 170,000 members answered the call and were renamed the National Volunteers. Many of these men would serve with great distinction in the 10th and 16th Irish Divisions and many other units of the British Army.

Those who remained, approximately 12,000, became a more militant entity and were dominated by the IRB and retained the title of the Irish Volunteers. They saw the ensuing European war as a means to an end and used the ideology that 'England's difficulty was Ireland's opportunity.' They formed a military council and enlisted many noted personalities including Patrick Pearse who would later be a protagonist in the 1916 Rebellion in Dublin. Although the Rebellion was to fail in its attempt it did however signal the Volunteers' determination and galvanised opinion, which would later resound through the War of Independence.

Pearse at the same meeting in the Rotunda Rink in 1913 said:

> *'The bearing of arms is not only the proudest right of citizenship, but it is the most essential duty, because the ability to enjoy the other duties of citizenship can only be guarded by the ability to defend citizenship.'*[4]

---

[4] G. White & B. O'Shea. *The Irish Volunteer Soldier*

Referring to the Home Rule debate he said:

> *'There are people in the hall who share the belief that for Ireland*
> *there can be no true freedom within the British Empire. There are*
> *doubtless, many more who believe that Ireland can achieve and*
> *enjoy very substantial freedom within the empire. But Ireland*
> *armed will, at any rate make a better bargain with the empire*
> *than Ireland unarmed.'*[5]

These beliefs were shared by many Irishmen who were later the backbone of the Volunteer movement. After the split with the Redmond-ites Parliamentary Party the more extreme nationalist minded element followed Pearse's and others radical leadership, which ultimately led to the 1916 Rebellion.

Later, with the rebellion collapsing, Pearse, the Commander-in-Chief of the Volunteers wrote a letter from the burning G.P.O. dated Friday, 28 April, 1916:

> *'I desire now, lest I may not have an opportunity later, to pay*
> *homage to the gallantry of the soldiers of Irish freedom who have*
> *during the past four days been writing with fire and steel the most*
> *glorious chapter in the later history of Ireland. Justice can never*
> *be done to their heroism, to their discipline, to their gay and*
> *unconquerable spirit in the midst of peril and death.'*[6]

The Easter Rebellion of 1916 was a testament to the fighting spirit and morale of the Irish Volunteers. The song that was sung by the garrisons of the Volunteers during the latter stages of the fighting was to become the National Anthem of the Irish Republic.

While recruitment became less visible immediately after the Easter Rebellion, the surge in public support for the movement after the executions of 1916 and prisoner releases of 1917 saw increased

[5] G White & B O'Shea *The Irish Volunteer Soldier 1913-23* pp 9-12
[6] G White & B O'Shea *The Irish Volunteer Soldier 1913-23* pp 9-12

numbers wishing to join. The British government threat of introducing conscription to Ireland in 1918 had a similar effect. Recruitment continued throughout the Anglo-Irish war, even after the ending of the First World War. From June 1920, recruits had to swear allegiance to Dáil Éireann and the Irish Republic.

The violence and political situation in Ireland took its toll and Lloyd George eventually offered a form of dominion status, limited by defence restrictions and maintaining partition in 1921. There was however more on offer than de Valera and the anti-Treaty-ites realised many years later. In the end the British invited Irish delegates to London with a view to 'ascertaining how the association of Ireland with the community of nations known as the British Empire may be reconciled with Irish national aspirations'. This meeting of the belligerents would see the negotiation and signing of the Anglo-Irish Treaty. The earlier signing of the Truce in July 1921, brought in more volunteers and later recruitment commenced for the National Army in January 1922, but there was dramatic divergence within the army as a result of differences over the Treaty. The Truce brought a stop to hostilities and prepared the ground for the Treaty negotiations, which set up the Irish Free State. The War of Independence had resulted in the deaths of around 405 RIC officers (many of whom were Catholic), 150 military personnel and approximately 750 IRA members and civilians.

On 5 July 1922, the Provisional Government issued a nationwide call to arms in an effort to attract new recruits, with dramatic effects. Many recruits were drawn from the ranks of the Irish Republican Army (Volunteers) and started taking over the vacated barracks from the departing British forces. This new army, established by Michael Collins, was planned as a conventional land force supported by a small air arm with a total strength of 4,000. The first appearance of the new force was in the form of the Dublin Guards, a composite unit of the IRA's Dublin brigade. They wore entirely new uniforms and were structured in a totally different manner.

In February 1922, the Department of Defence under the new Provisional government began to recruit volunteers for the regular army. Properly uniformed and equipped, this unit marched past Michael Collins at Dublin City Hall en route to take over the vacated British barracks at Beggars Bush. By this time about 3,500 men had enlisted as a consequence of the looming Civil War and would eventually reach 55,000 by its violent conclusion.

When the Dáil approved the Treaty on 7 January 1922, the majority was only 64 to 57 votes and disharmony began to foster. Many members of the IRA, which Collins had led, were unhappy with the terms of the Treaty, believing that they should fight on for a fully independent all Ireland Republic. This was the atmosphere in which the new National Army was recruited. The army, to all intents and purposes, had no sooner emerged from a successful guerrilla campaign with an external enemy than it was asked to fight a conventional campaign in a bitter Civil War. Each side in the conflict whereby the original volunteers split maintained that they were the true IRA and depending on their allegiance, they were labelled the National or Free State Army or Regulars on the one hand and Republicans, anti-Treaty or Irregulars on the other. On 14 April 1922, the Irregulars took over the Four Courts complex on the north bank of the River Liffey and set up head quarters there.

On 15 June the pro-Treaty faction won a general election and negotiations came to a halt with the Four Courts garrisons. At 4 a.m. on the morning of 28 June, the guns of the Free State National Army opened up from the South bank of the river, signalling the beginning of the Irish Civil War. The Civil War turned out to be an untidy one, without clear-cut agendas at the beginning or the end. This was a conflict for which neither side had prepared. Before the conflict came to an end, Chiefs of Staff on each side would be killed in action as would many other high profile members and rank and file alike.

To prevent the country from slipping into total anarchy the government gave the National Army increased powers including the establishment of military courts that could enforce the death sentence on those taken under arms after an amnesty. As a result the National Army executed seventy-seven 'Irregular' prisoners and this caused bitter enmity between the former comrades, which lasted for generations. After regular successes of the army in the field against the Irregulars and the death in action of their Chief of Staff Liam Lynch in April 1923, his successor Frank Aiken ordered an end to hostilities. The Irregulars had realised they had lost the support of the people and could not win the war at that time. The war was over. The National Army was victorious but at a great price. The deep wounds of Civil War would not be healed for many generations. The National Army had not yet known what it was like to be a regular peacetime army and on 3 August 1923 the Defence Forces (Temporary Provisions) Act 1923 finally put it on a statutory footing.

The demobilisation of the 'Civil War National Army' started in the autumn of 1923, and in February 1924 a memorandum set out its planned evolution into a regular army. Óglaigh na hÉireann had had its baptism of fire in 1916, it evolved through a learning process during the War of Independence and it survived the ultimate test of Civil War. Now it was to be subordinate to the primacy of politics, it would have to evolve and learn even more. For the first time in seven and a half centuries Ireland was to have a regular peacetime army and it was about to undergo an internal struggle.

In 1923, there were rumblings beneath the surface, which ended in a series of incidents amounting to mutiny by a group of officers, two of which were Major General Tom Cullen and Major General Liam Tobin, both were senior Aides de Comp to the Governor General. Some of these officers had been close associates of Michael Collins, several had been members of the Dublin Volunteers active service unit, had served with distinction against the British forces and had borne the brunt of the fighting during the War of Independence. After the war they were unhappy with their appointments and lowered status. They protested that the government was not interpreting the Treaty in accordance with Collins' stepping stone theory. They formed their own organisation within the army, the Old IRA Group, in order to wrest control of the force and use it to achieve political and personal objectives. They disapproved of officers who had held commissions in the British Army and declared that they wanted to be involved with the plans to demobilise the Irish force. They also wanted to keep elements of their own organisations within that force.

At the same time the Irish Republican Brotherhood (IRB) was being reorganised under the army council by the Quarter Master General, Sean Ó Muirthile, in order to prevent it falling into the hands of the Irregulars. It had been dormant since the signing of the Treaty but was still a tool to be used. The members of the previous group were unwelcome and animosity grew between the two. Things were to come to a head with the proposal to reduce the May 1923 army strength of 55,000 troops to 31,500 by January 1924. The demobilisation of officers presented a particular problem. There were three categories listed for dismissal: (a) unsuitable officers (b) post-Truce officers who had no special qualifications and (c) pre-Truce officers who were surplus to requirements. Things boiled over in September 1923 when a Defence Order was issued providing advance notice of demobilisation of officers.

Anger at this manifested itself in many ways but one event in Collins Barracks Dublin saw a portrait of Michael Collins being smashed and burned in the middle of the square as a protest by disgruntled officers. As they saw it, the wrong men were being kept on, while they, who had done all the fighting, were being dismissed. They formed their own IRA Organisation (IRAO).

This demobilisation meant drastic reductions in troop numbers including the provision of a force of 1,300 officers and 18,000 men. This meant the dismissal of 2,000 officers and 27,000 men from its maximum strength. Many officers refused to accept their demobilisation papers. They were charged with insubordination, convicted by court-martial and sentenced to dismissal. But this was not followed through and a new trial was ordered. However, eventually, the officers yielded to persuasion and left the forces. Some others felt that they had got away with it and it was later judged to have been prejudicial to good order and discipline. The tensions between the rival organisations within the army began to mount. Matters came to a head again on 6 March 1924 when Major General Liam Tobin and Colonel Charles Dalton delivered an ultimatum to the government on behalf of the Old IRA Group of officers. (Dalton was a brother of General Emmet Dalton, an ex-British soldier, IRA and National Army veteran).

They demanded an immediate conference with the government to discuss the interpretation of the Treaty on the following conditions: removal of the army council and immediate suspension of demobilisation. The government responded by ordering the arrest of both men, but they managed to escape.

The following day 900 officers were demobilised without incident. Certain officers however, who had not been demobilised began to leave the army in an irregular fashion. Two deserted Gormanston Camp, taking with them a Crossly Tender and some weapons, ammunition and equipment. Three left Baldonnel with another Crossly Tender and three Lewis machine guns amongst other war material. In all, over fifty officers absconded taking material with them, and forty-nine others, including three Major Generals and five Colonels, resigned. Many tendered their resignations in protest. Their view was that freedom fighters were being dismissed while ex-British officers and soldiers were being retained. Irish soldiers of the War of

Independence and Civil War period would not have had the experience of a conventional army like those who would have had service in the British Army. It would have made sense to try and retain ex-British soldiers as a nucleus of experience around which to build an army. But it was personality clashes and losses of position, power and prestige at a time of high unemployment, which were the main factors causing the dissatisfaction. This dissatisfaction caused serious disobedience in March 1924.

In the months that followed the Civil War it was not the civil unrest that was the greatest threat to the government but unrest within the army. The army had mutinied. Increasingly strained relations within the executive council between General Mulcahy and most of his colleagues complicated the government's handling of the army. Mulcahy was the person most criticised all through the war and after the collapse of the Irregulars. Kevin O'Higgins castigated the army for its indiscipline and performance and the rest of the government didn't disagree. This left Mulcahy weak when dealing with the malcontents such as Tobin, who scorned the army for the reasons outlined earlier and accused it of incompetence and being full of British spies. They were further outraged by Mulcahy's attempt to use the IRB as a focus of loyalty to the government from within the army. Reliance on a secret, oath-bound society within the army was disloyal and a threat and has had repercussions for the Irish Defence Forces ever since.

In the end, after all the strife, a purge was carried out within the army and among the Military Council. The highest-ranking victim, although he resigned when requested to do so by O'Higgins, was General Mulcahy. Mulcahy had always enforced the ideal that the civil government should be the sole controller of the country's armed forces and Eunan O'hAlpín (1999) recognises his resignation as being detrimental to the army. The civilians in the Department of Defence saw his resignation and that of others as an admission of guilt and justified their purges of the Army Council. The result of the mutiny and its aftermath was to have a serious effect on how the army was handled and financed for many years.

Mulcahy was eventually exonerated of the main assertions made against him but it came too late and the government suffered no embarrassment. The army was never given the finance, policy or power to be considered a formidable entity again, in a way paying the price for the manner of its conception.

Between 1913 and 1924, the Irish Army went through a period of transition from volunteerism to mutiny. Its evolvement as a national and nationalist tool was precarious indeed and one can see that its survival at all was not without luck. The Irish War of Independence seemed to bond together the elements that made up this fighting force but it was the Irish Civil War and mutiny of 1924 that were almost its undoing.

The memories of what happened during the period formed a constrictive boundary on the army's development. Not only the terrible things that happened during the Civil War between old comrades but the perceived disloyalty and mutiny of the post war army had helped to convince some politicians to judge it as untrustworthy. The army however was fighting for the elected government and its victory ensured the commencement and survival of a democratic government in Ireland. It is vitally important to acknowledge that amongst all those who fought for Irish independence were British trained Irishmen who helped revolutionise the Irish Army and they also fought and died for the promise and ideals of Ireland.

John Redmond at Volunteer meeting. *Courtesy of the National Library of Ireland.*

WRAF at Tallaght Aerodrome. *South Dublin Libraries Local Studies Collection.*

Easter Rebellion 1916.
South Dublin Libraries Local Studies Collection.

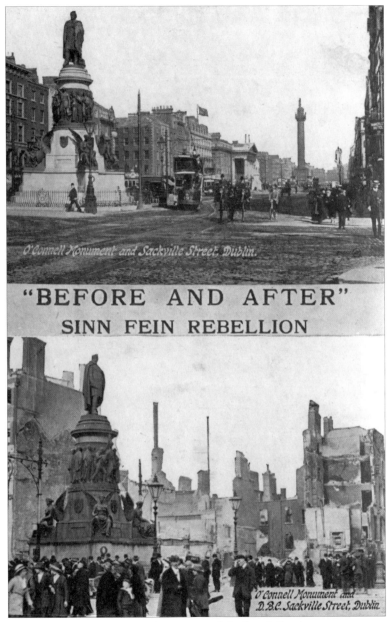

South Dublin Libraries Local Studies Collection.

'these men would go down in history as heroes and martyrs
and I will go down, if I go down at all,
as a bloody English officer'

Tom Kettle 1916, *Irish Nationalist Killed WWI*

Chapter II

INDEPENDENCE AND HOMECOMING 1913-1921

THE GOAL POSTS MOVE

'Let me say plainly that if any Irishman is convinced that he will
serve Ireland by becoming a British soldier, and if he acts on
that conviction, he is a patriotic and brave man. If any Irishman
thinks sincerely that Mr Redmond is entitled to be the keeper of
his political conscience, and that he serves Ireland by following
Mr Redmond's advice without reserve, and if for that reason he
becomes a British soldier, he is a brave man.'

Eoin McNeill, February 1916[7]

PRIOR to 1922 there was already a long tradition of Irishmen
serving in the military forces of Britain. In 1830 Irishmen
represented forty two percent of the British Army at a time when
Ireland accounted for approximately one third of the total population
of the United Kingdom. Between 1825 and 1850 forty eight percent of
the Bengal Army of the East India Company was Irish.[8] The famous
Republican, United Irishman and 1798 Rebellion leader Theobold

---

[7]Ben Novick, *Conceiving Revolution, Irish Nationalist Propaganda During the First World War,* (Dublin, 2001), p.60

[8]Alvin Jackson, Ireland, 'The Union and the Empire 1800-1960', in Kevin Kenny, ed., *Ireland and the British Empire: Oxford history of the British Empire companion series.* (Oxford, 2004), p.141

Wolfe Tone had, in his early days, long thought of joining this same company as he liked the uniform and the idea of a soldier's life. There was never a shortage of Irish soldiers to man British colonial garrisons around the world or to fight in its many resulting wars. Those who joined the army did so for a myriad of reasons, which included adventurism, patriotism and economics. The artist Lady Elizabeth Butler, who painted the well-known portrayal of a recruitment scene in the painting 'Listed for the Connaughts' in 1878, believed that enlistment in the British Army was a solution to the poverty of Western Ireland. Many generations of Irish families had proud attachments to the British Army even though Ireland had a rebellious tradition of its own. During the Battle of Dundee, in the South African Boer War, Irish soldiers of the 2nd Battalion of the Royal Dublin Fusiliers found themselves in action against Irishmen of the Boer Irish Transvaal Brigade. The Boer Army consisted in part of an estimated 1,200 Irishmen who had joined in disgust at the treatment of the Boers "small nation" by the British. The following verse is from an anonymous ballad, which refers to the Irish involvement on both sides and centres around one of the many battles where Irishmen fought each other.

On the mountain side the battle raged, there was no stop or stay;
Mackin captured Private Burke and Ensign Michael Shea,
FitzGerald got FitzPatrick, Brannigan found O'Rourke;
Finnegan took a man named Fay — and a couple of lads from Cork.
Suddenly they heard McManus shout, "Hands up or I'll run you through".
He thought it was a Yorkshire "tyke" — twas Corporal Donaghue!
McGarry took O'Leary, O'Brien got McNamee,
That's how the "English fought the Dutch" at the Battle of Dundee.[9]

---

[9]From speech notes delivered by Mr Sean Connolly at the centenary celebrations of the Royal Dublin Fusiliers memorial arch in Stephens Green, Dublin on 19 August 2007, the action was also known as the Battle of Talana Hill.

There was already a considerable anti-British current in Dublin in the late 1890s but most moderate nationalists abhorred the use of violence and did not wish to see Ireland break its ties with Britain. However, the war had a considerable effect on those in Ireland who supported the campaign for Home Rule and a committee was set up to support the liberties of the Transvaal against British oppression. This committee included Arthur Griffith, James Connolly, Willie Redmond, Michael Davitt and other high profile personalities. Constitutional nationalists preferred to see Ireland with its own parliament making decisions affecting Ireland's internal government like education, health and agriculture while Westminster would deal with issues like trade and defence. This could be achieved through the implementation of Home Rule.

The example of the small Boer nation challenging the might of the British Empire and winning victories would encourage those who later instigated armed rebellion in Ireland. But even after all this when the Great War began Irishmen from both sides in the Boer War fought against Germany in British uniforms. All during the 1919-1921 War in Ireland recruitment of Irishmen to the British Army continued and even escalated. Poverty and social conditions were probably the main reasons for Irishmen making careers through service to the Crown, their primary loyalties being to themselves, their families and their religion and then the local community and to Ireland. Irish society at a certain level had militarised elements prior to Independence and so before 1914 the Volunteers would have had experienced people on which to rely. Between 1913 and 1924 the Irish army developed from a volunteer force to a guerrilla force during the Irish War of Independence and through to a semi-conventional army during the Irish Civil War, all the time utilising the skills of British ex-servicemen.

The formation of the Volunteers was a direct result of the proposed Third Home Rule Bill, which was introduced in 1912 but later shelved on the statute books until after the First World War. Time after time in the course of the Irish Revolution radical Nationalists had followed the example provided by Ulster Unionists and elements within the British Army.[10] The Irish Volunteers had modelled themselves on the Ulster Volunteer Force, which had earlier been founded to defend Ulster against Home Rule in Ireland. Both relied on the experience of ex-British soldiers to militarise their forces. A confidential monthly report of the Inspector General for January 1913 to the Under Secretary for Ireland reveals some of the tensions.

> *'In Belfast and Northern Ulster the Home Rule Bill continues to be regarded by unionists with apprehension and bitter hostility. A body called the Ulster Volunteer Force is being raised. It is said that the volunteers will furnish a police as well as a military force for service under a 'Provisional Government' to be established for Ulster in the event of the Home Rule Bill becoming law'.*[11]

Many areas such as Antrim had a noticeable increase in the number of unionist clubs and drilling and route marches with members being taught to use firearms.[12] The Orange Order had taken up the UVF movement by May 1913 and urged its members to join, with the cities being divided up into sections over which commanders were appointed in order to quickly mobilise the force.[13] The country gentry inspected drill and parades; many of them were retired military officers and appeared, according to a police report, to be at the head of the movement.[14] By July 1913 a county inspector's report estimated that

[10]Michael Laffan, *The Resurrection of Ireland, the Sinn Féin Party 1916-1923* (New York, 2005), p.411

[11]County Inspectors report, January 1913, Colonial Office papers CO904, British in Ireland series (Held in British National Archives but available on microfilm at NUI Maynooth AS941.5, box 89 reel 054), pp 1-9

[12]County Inspector's report 13 May 1913, CO904

[13]Ibid, p.10

[14]Ibid, The strength of the UVF at this stage was thought to be somewhere in the region of 30,000 men

there were 7,000 fairly well drilled men in the Antrim UVF indicating an alarming slide toward a militant society.[15] A police sergeant in Hollywood, Co Down reported parties of the Ulster force practicing signalling, despatch carrying, scouting, skirmishing, ambulance drill, tent pitching and coding. Captain F. Hall and ex-sergeant Jeffreys of the Royal Irish Regiment, W.G. Ferguson, an ex-Sergeant and ex-Quartermaster Sergeant W.F. Maxwell, late of the Royal Irish Regiment, judged other units.[16] Sir George Richards a retired English Lt. Colonel who had settled in Ireland was appointed the UVF Commander in Chief. His headquarters were in Belfast's old town hall and consisted of army officers organising a comprehensive system of intelligence, communications and best military practice.[17] The UVF was organised to coordinate paramilitary resistance among Northern unionists. No attempt was made to prevent the distribution of arms after the Larne gun running of April 1914 and the Curragh mutiny in March.

The Irish Citizen Army (ICA), Irish Volunteers and later the IRA also used men with military combat experience. Men like Tom Byrne who had fought against the British with the Irish Brigade in South Africa during the Boer War.[18] Professional soldiers, for example, like Colonel Maurice Moore and Colonel Edmund Cotter and a number of ex-British NCOs gave their services free of charge as directors of military organisation officers and drill instructors to the Volunteers.[19]

---

[15]Ibid, pp 389-392, in Fermanagh there was 1,246 men, Londonderry there was 3,349 men, Monahan had 700 and Tyrone had 3,300 drilled men

[16]RIC special branch report on secret societies 14 August 1913 to Undersecretary Neville Chamberlain Colonial Office papers CO 904, p.398

[17]F.X. Martin & F.J. Byrne, pp 104-5

[18]Tom Byrne was member of Irish brigade in South Africa 1900-02, a captain in the I.V. in 1916 and commandant in the IRA in Dublin 1921 BMH NAI WS 564

[19]F.X. Martin & F.J. Byrne, p.141

Moore was a descendent of a well-known Irish Catholic family, which had managed to retain their lands in Co. Mayo. He had trained in Sandhurst Military College and was commissioned into the Connaught Rangers in 1875, fought in the Kaffir and Zulu Wars 1877-1879 and also in Natal. He commanded the 1st Battalion Connaught Rangers 1900-1906 and formed a cavalry corps, which distinguished itself during the Boer War. Later he became a strong supporter of John Redmond and his Parliamentary Party and during the Free State period he campaigned for the withholding of land annuities, he was appointed as envoy of Dáil Éireann to France in 1922 and was a founder member of the Fianna Fáil Party in 1926.[20]

The most able instructors to the UVF and the Irish Volunteers were themselves products of the British Army.[21] After the formation of the Irish Volunteers in 1913 emphasis was put on the training of its members, which would be needed in any struggle to defend Home Rule or Independence.[22] Indeed, the need for these skills and the probable cognisance of what was happening in the North led to military instructions being issued for units of the Volunteers in 1914 to establish along British army lines. They were to secure the services of a competent instructor utilising all ex-military men where possible and the company drill was to follow exactly the drill set out in the British Infantry Manual 1911.[23]

---

[20]Hayes Catalogue Vol. 10, 1700-1960 Ms. 10,561 Col Maurice Moore papers NLI, Col. Maurice Moore 1854-1939 in D.J. Hickey & J.F. Doherty, *A Dictionary of Irish History 1800-1980* (Dublin, 1987), p.112

[21]Captain Barry O' Brien, 'The origins and development of the Cadet school 1929-1979, in *A Special Edition of the An Cosantor, The Irish Defence Journal,* vol. xxxix no. 9 (Dublin, 1979), p.260

[22]*Musketry and Training in the Dublin Volunteers,* Walsh Papers, NLI, n.4923

[23]Bulmer Hobson Papers, NLI, MS. 13174 (1)

In 1914, the Cork City Corps of Irish Volunteers was looking for someone with sufficient military experience to train its units to a high level of military proficiency. In May of that year Captain Maurice Talbot Crosbie, a retired British artillery officer from Ardfert in County Kerry, offered his services. After attending a drill meeting on Sunday 24 May, Crosbie joined the Cork City Irish Volunteers and by the end of the day he had been appointed as its commanding officer. With Crosbie in control of the military functions of the corps the rest of the Volunteer leadership could concentrate on improving other aspects of the countrywide movement.[24]

However, Crosbie was a loyal Redmondite and would later come into conflict with the Volunteer leadership when he offered the Cork units to the British government to defend Ireland during the First World War. This was above his remit as a corps commander and was not on the agenda of the republican volunteer leadership and came to a head during the Volunteer split in 1914 when the fragmentation of the rank and file became apparent.[25]

The Irish Citizen Army was formed on 23 November 1913, as a result of the now famous lockout of that year, to defend unemployed and striking workers. Its first commander was Captain Jack White, an Ulster Protestant and son of a distinguished British Field-Marshal Sir George White, the defender of Ladysmith during the Boer War and who was also Commander in Chief in India between 1893 and 1897. Captain White had won the Distinguished Service Order (DSO) while fighting with the Gordon Highlanders during the Boer War.[26] Other senior members within the ICA with British service included Michael Mallin and James Connolly, but like the Volunteers the movements became professional and disciplined.

---

[24]Gerry White & Brendan O'Shea, *Baptised in Blood: the Formation of the Cork Brigade of the Irish Volunteers 1913-1916,* p.34

[25]Ibid, pp 34-47

[26]F.X. Martin & F.J. Byrne, pp 122 & 138

When the insurrection occurred in 1916 the Volunteers were said to have conducted themselves in a professional and soldier-like fashion. Captain E. Gerard of the British Army said 'every officer I ever met who was ever in Dublin was so impressed by the extraordinary gallant behaviour of the insurgents.'[27] Prior to 1916, and although seeking a non-violent approach, Bulmer Hobson referred to the British Army and the excellent source of military skills that men trained in that institution might provide. He proposed the utilisation of ex-British soldiers and the British military manual to train the Volunteers for the eventual fight with Britain.[28] As a result groups of this type of persuasion of men formed together by 1914 and

'An intensive training course of drilling, route marches and rifle practice were carried out during the summer... In fact our drilling exercises were carried out on the Curragh and often witnessed by officers and men of the British army. A number of British ex army men, living in the district acted as instructors and one of them, William Jones, was an ex corporal of the Connaught Rangers and a first class drill instructor. On the out break of war in August 1914 nearly all the drill instructors were called up as they were on reserve of the British army including William Jones but by that time a number of our own men were qualified to carry out the training of the company'.[29]

Like Martin Byrne who was a drill instructor to the Carlow brigade during the Tan War, Jones was repatriated to Ireland as a result of injuries received in France and he again joined the IRA. He was employed in the Curragh camp but was arrested in September 1915 under the Defence of the Realm Act (DORA). This was an emergency

---

[27]Captain E. Gerard ADC 5th division British forces in Ireland 1916-21 defended Beggars Bush barracks 1916, BMH, NA, WS 34800
[28]Bulmer Hobson papers, NLI, MS. 13174
[29]James Durney, *On the one road: political unrest in Kildare 1913-1994* (Naas, 2001), p.13

act passed in 1914 to prevent collaboration between Irish separatists and Germany. Jones lost his job and his army pension and then set about training the Volunteers with greater enthusiasm.[30]

First World War, Rebellion and Ex-Servicemen

The advent of World War One put on hold the escalation towards Civil War in Ireland. Soon after the outbreak of war with Germany, which was declared on 4 August 1914, the Irish Parliamentary Party offered the Irish Volunteers to the Crown in defence of Ireland, partly to safeguard Home Rule and partly in response to Carson offering the UVF to fight in the war. It is important to remember that when Europe went to war, Ireland as part of the British Empire was automatically involved. 150,000 Irishmen immediately volunteered to fight. The British Expeditionary Force included four Irish cavalry regiments and nine Irish infantry battalions sent to Belgium with thousands of Irish in other English units.

The Home Rule Bill was signed by King George on 18 September and placed on the statute books but was suspended until after the war. Soon afterwards John Redmond, John Dillon and Joseph Devlin had negotiations with Herbert Asquith, the British Prime Minister, in a recruitment meeting at the Mansion House in Dublin. Redmond's offer had taken place without any real consultation or consensus with the Volunteer leadership on the ground and was evident also of the power struggle going on within the movement. But there was enthusiasm for the war, recruitment figures showed that Ireland was in the grip of a war fever and, according to some, Redmond was in the driving seat. Some 43,000 men had enlisted between August and December of that year. It was from the working classes and most underprivileged of the industrialised urban centres that recruits would step forth.[31]

[30]Ibid, p.16
[31]Jerome Aan De Weil, 'Archbishop Walsh and Mgr. Curran's opposition to the British war effort in Dublin 1914-1918', in *The Irish Sword: The journal of the military history society of Ireland,* Vol. XXII, No 88, (Dublin, 2000), p.194

However, the advent of the First World War also saw the split in the Irish Volunteer movement, which by this time had reached 180,000 members. The larger portion of 170,000 sided with Redmond and the Nationalist Parliamentary Party and became the National Volunteers, many of whom later fought in the Great War. On 20 September 1914, John Redmond appealed to the Volunteers gathered at a rally in Woodenbridge, Co. Wicklow to take part in the war. He said that the time had come for them to account for themselves as men, not only in Ireland itself but wherever the firing line extends, in defence of right of freedom and religion in this war. Many Irishmen listened and responded to his words.

The Irish War of Independence or Anglo-Irish War came about at the end of nearly ten years of intense political and armed activity. But it began because confidence in Redmondite constitutionalism had come to an end and because of Sinn Féin's election success in 1918. John Redmond, the Parliamentary Party leader and Charles Stewart Parnell's political successor, had managed to lead and hold together a united party while holding the balance of power in the House of Commons, forcing the British Prime Minister Herbert Asquith to introduce a Home Rule Bill in 1912. Like the earlier constitutionalists, Redmond tried to avoid armed uprising believing this would harm Ireland considerably more than it would Britain He understood the strength of Ulster Unionists and their resistance to the proposed introduction of Home Rule. Some of those in opposition to the war saw the nationalist party as no longer serving Ireland but their masters, the English Liberals and this view was justified by the offer to commit Irishmen to the war with Germany.

Today there is considerably more interest in the service of those men who served in the Great War than at any other time, especially from academics and historians. The period can now safely be revisited and interpreted. Hundreds of thousands of Irish soldiers enlisted for a multitude of social and economic reasons but fundamentally in the service of a sovereign and free Ireland. They too were Irish soldiers fighting for their homes, their families and their comrades. They fought through the carnage and most massive bloodletting in history, through the battles and the terror of Gallipoli, the Somme, Ypres, Messines, and Passchendaele, for the promise of liberty for Ireland.

On the outbreak of hostilities 30,266 reservists reported directly to their depots and a total of 140,460 men enlisted in Ireland during the war.[32] By January 1918 the National Volunteers and the UVF had provided almost 45% of the 141,528 recruits and reservists, which as Patrick Callan rightly points out, underlies the importance of the recruiting campaigns for the Irish brigades by the Irish Parliamentary Party and likewise for the 36th Ulster Division by the Unionist Party.[33] But as Callan also states an amazing 95% of the volunteer total enlisted prior to 1916 with the political profile fading after the Rising.[34] In Nationalist circles the idealistic view that the war was for small nations, freedom and democracy soon wilted.

The smaller group of Volunteers, that did not follow Redmond after the 1914 split, became the nucleus of the movement that produced the rebellion of 1916 and the War of Independence. This group retained the title of Irish Volunteers and subscribed to the ideology that England's difficulty was Ireland's opportunity. The Provisional Committee of the Irish Volunteers was formed in Wynn's Hotel on 11 November 1913. The Volunteers themselves were inaugurated in the Rotunda Rink in Dublin on 25 November and immediately began placing a precise form of military structure on the organisation. Volunteer units were called 'corps', 'brigades' or 'regiments', traditional standing army formation titles. When the first convention of

---

[32]Patrick Callan, 'Recruiting in the British army in Ireland during the First World War'
in *The Irish sword: the journal of the military history society of Ireland* (Dublin, 1987),
pp 42-56
[33]Ibid
[34]Ibid

the Irish Volunteers assembled in Dublin on 25 October 1914, it was decided to govern the movement with both general and executive councils.[35]

A committee of military organisations was appointed and tasked with drafting a proposal for the establishment of a General Head Quarters (GHQ). These proposals, which were endorsed by both the Central Executive and General Council allowed for the establishment of a GHQ staff comprising a chief of staff, a quartermaster general and directors of organisations, military operations, training and arms and later a chief of inspection and director of communications.[36]

GHQ was responsible for the overall operations of the Irish Volunteers until the establishment of the National Army in 1922. 1914 also saw the adaptation of the scheme of military organisation, which saw the main volunteer tactical unit designated as a 'company'. The scheme also provided for the establishment of engineer, transport, supply and communications and hospital corps. Volunteer brigades were commanded by a general and consisted of three to five battalions. The Volunteers utilised the British military manual and system and this would follow through to the Irish War of Independence and Civil War.

By 1915 many former members of the Irish Volunteers had taken part in the actions at Gallipoli and various other places wearing British uniforms, while fighting for the Crown, the freedom of small nations and the promise of a form of Irish freedom. While Irish soldiers serving in France were preparing for the great Somme offensive of 1916, back home in Ireland the Irish Volunteers, in a bid for independence but mostly to empower a new generation and a new era of separatist revival, instigated the Easter rebellion. By this time Roger Casement had already recruited some Irish prisoners of war from various camps like the Lemberg POW camp in Germany, albeit with minimal success, to form an Irish Brigade for the sole purpose of

[35]Gerry White and Brendan O' Shea, 'Irish volunteer soldier 1913-23',
  in *Osprey Warrior Series no. 80* (Oxford, 2003), pp 8-13
[36]Ibid

fighting the British in Ireland. He recruited only fifty-two men. Many prisoners especially those long serving men like Lance Sergeant William O'Reilly of the 1st Battalion of the Royal Irish Fusiliers, who had been active from the beginning of the war were quite hostile and rebuffed Casement.

O'Reilly had joined the British Army just after the turn of the century serving in India and after his pre war service but before his actual war time service he managed to come home for a brief spell, get married and father a child whom he would never meet. His wife died soon after the child's birth in 1914. William O'Reilly also perished in 1917 from injuries received earlier in battle; he had spent over three years in captivity. He had earlier trained the local Volunteers.[37]

One of those Casement did manage to recruit was a man named Corporal Timothy Quinlisk who joined Sinn Féin but was later found to be a spy and executed on the orders of Michael Collins. In his last message to the Irish people Casement wrote, in a highly utilised piece of propaganda, 'I cast no stone at the millions of brave dead throughout Europe-God rest their souls in peace.'[38]

Michael Kehoe, another POW and the brigade's adjutant, was recruited and later fought in the Irish War of Independence, as did Maurice Meade, later a section commander in the East Limerick flying column and national army during the Civil War.[39] Private Thomas Higgins, Fair Green, Naas had been captured during the Battle of Mons while serving with the 2nd Royal Dublin Fusiliers. He was at Lemberg POW camp on the day Sir Roger Casement visited and said *'it is time to strike a blow for Ireland'*.

---

[37]Myles Dungan, *They Shall Grow Not Old: Irish Soldiers and the Great War,* (Dublin, 1997), pp 154-162; also from authors correspondence with Eilish Lambe, Grand-daughter of William O' Reilly
[38]Ben Novick, p.69
[39]Michael J. Kehoe, WS 741 BMH NAI; Maurice Meade, WS 891 BMH NAI

Higgins reminisced:

> *We were then told that an Irish brigade was to be formed from amongst the prisoners. We were to be given uniforms of green with shamrocks as collar badges. We were to be equipped and fitted out in every way to fight for Ireland. They took the precaution of meeting an objection that would occur to many of us even supposing we were willing to become traitors to our empire.*

They told us: *If you join the Irish Brigade and the Germans win the war they will land the Irish Brigade in Ireland to free Ireland, and send some Germans troops to reinforce you. If the Germans do not win the war we will give you £20 each, send you to America and guarantee you employment there with German firms.*

We booed Sir Roger Casement out of the camp…[40]

While the 16th (Irish) Division, John Redmond's so called Irish Brigades suffered massive casualties as a result of gas attacks at Hulluch on 27 and 29 April 1916, Irish soldiers in Ireland were dying while fighting each other on the streets of Dublin. The rebel army fought soldiers of the very army who would provide them in the future with military experience of a conventional force. Some historians see this event as Ireland's first Civil War of the twentieth century and others as just another battle of the Great War. The Rising in a sense brought the conflict straight home to Ireland with the main city almost destroyed by modern weapons of war.[41]

The initial days of the insurrection took the government and military by surprise. In many parts of Dublin sympathy was not with the rebels. British soldiers and especially Irishmen serving in the British Army up until this point had held a level of respect in the country. With the outbreak of war in Europe this was compounded by the fact that many Irishmen were now fighting in that war. There were far too many

---

[40]James Durney, p.18
[41]Ben Novick, p.64

Dubliners fighting with Irish regiments in France for the population to think that this was the right moment to embarrass England.[42] Ben Novick's excellent study of Irish nationalist propaganda during World War One reveals the complete shift in advanced nationalist propaganda towards Irish troops serving in the British army during the war both before and after the carnage of Gallipoli in 1915 and especially the 1916 Rebellion. Earlier on, soldiers heading off to the front bore the brunt of nationalist scorn even from the likes of James Connolly when he wrote 'Let the wastrels go, let the dupes go — Ireland is well rid of them.'

When war had broken out in 1914 advanced nationalist attitudes reflected pre-war anti-recruitment propaganda but as the casualties mounted as with the destruction of the volunteer 10th Division in the Dardanelle's, public opinion as a whole turned against the war but public sympathy and support for Irish soldiers remained.[43] Once Irish soldiers began to be involved in serious combat, with its resultant killed and maimed, harsh mockery disappeared. According to Novick the worst that was said of them was that they were misguided fools who had been tricked into volunteering for certain death by recruiters.

Connolly declared of the soldiers, 'these poor misguided brothers of ours...who had been tricked and deluded into giving battle for England.' Most sympathetic voices came from 1915 and 1916 and right up until the eve of the Easter Rebellion.[44] Before the 1916 Rising, with the early carnage and loss of the war, the majority of writings showed true pity and sympathy for the men suffering at the front remembering that many had once been Irish Volunteers. A form of respect even extended to British-born soldiers.[45] Ex-soldiers also fought with the Volunteers against their old comrades in British uniform during 1916 and some later wrote of their experiences.

---

[42]Desmond Bowen and Jean Bowen, *Heroic option: The Irish in the British army* (Yorkshire, 2005), pp 242-44
[43]Ben Novick, pp 56-7
[44]Ibid, pp 58-9
[45]Ibid, p.63

W. J. Brennan Whitmore was born in Wexford in 1886 and joined the British Army, serving with the Royal Irish Regiment and the medical corps as a sergeant in India. After returning to Wexford in 1907 he became involved with Arthur Griffith and the Sinn Féin and Gaelic League movements and joined the Volunteers in 1913. Using his military background he became involved in organising the Volunteers in the South East and later became Officer Commanding the Ferns Company and later adjutant to the North Wexford Brigade. He was introduced to the national leadership of the Volunteers through Ginger O'Connell and was keen to train volunteers, properly pushing the idea of tactics suited to the Irish terrain rather than replicating the British model. Later he was appointed to the General Staff of the Volunteers and produced a training manual incorporating his ideas. He was a general staff officer in the GPO and Director of Field Intelligence in 1916 before taking command of the North Earl St. positions during the battle for Dublin. While imprisoned in Frongoch he was elected camp adjutant and prepared and secretly delivered lectures to senior officers on the application of general principles of military strategy on tactics to the Irish terrain. On return to Ireland he remained active in the nationalist movement, working as an intelligence officer on Michael Collins' staff. During the Civil War he was based in the National Army head quarters as a staff officer with army intelligence and later succeeded Piaras Beaslaí as editor of the National Army's newspaper *An tÓglach*.[46]

The battles of Easter week were a military failure. Irish Volunteers had fought and killed Irish soldiers and ex-members of the Volunteers who now wore British uniforms. Many on the rebel side including some of the executed leaders had relatives in the army and in some cases it was brother against brother. Some of those same British soldiers of Irish regiments had been active in the Howth gun running operation two years previous. But after a week of intense fighting and the execution

---

[46]W.J. Brennan Whitmore, *Dublin burning: the Easter Rising from behind the Barricades,* (Dublin, 1996), pp ix-xv

of the rebel leaders public opinion saw the Rising as something to be proud of. Albert Resborough, a British soldier at the time, said that 'the army had respect for the Volunteers they were fighting as they saw them as very professional and disciplined'.[47] But many Irish soldiers serving at the front on hearing of the rebellion felt a greater sense of betrayal than patriotism. The soldiers of the 2nd Irish Guards were supporters of Home Rule but were not sympathetic towards the rebels. They, after all believed they were fighting for Ireland. Tom Kettle, a British officer at the time, wrote that he was astounded at the news of the rebellion. Many of the leaders had been his friends and he himself was a nationalist. Afterwards he said of the executions 'these men would go down in history as heroes and martyrs and I will go down if I go down at all as a bloody English officer'.[48]

Many others felt nothing for what had happened in Ireland as they were probably focussed on surviving the hostile front lines. Up until the time of the Rising in 1916 the public and the media had sympathised with the Irish soldier's plight at the front. From Gallipolli onwards the mass deaths of Irishmen had been a focus of the advanced nationalists in their hatred for the war with daily accounts of the actions. After the Rising the propagandists changed tactics. The Somme battles which occurred during the summer and autumn of 1916 passed without a mention as Irish regiments North and South engaged in some of the worst fighting yet seen, with many thousands of casualties.[49] In fact the old adage that soldiers die but battalions survive was true in the Irish case. In August 1914 the 2nd Battalion of the Royal Munster Fusiliers was thrown into the fight in France. Many of the old soldiers were soon killed or taken prisoner, their replacements died at the battles of 1915 and their replacements in 1917 and 1918. By November 1918 very few if any of the soldiers of 1914 remained in the battalion.[50]

---

[47]Albert George Fletcher Resborough, BMH NAI MAI WS 1604
[48]Bowen, p.244
[49]Novick, p.65
[50]From 'Soldiers and Chief's' exhibition National Museum of Ireland

In August 1915, less than a year after being formed, the 10th Irish Division commanded by Irishman Bryan McMahon landed at Suvla Bay on the Gallipoli peninsula. Poor staff work, inaccurate intelligence and piecemeal commitment of the division created chaos on the beaches. The division was essentially destroyed within two months.[51]

In September 1916 as part of the drawn out campaign of the Somme offensive the 16th Irish Division took the village of Ginchy at a cost of 4,000 dead and wounded. Among the dead was the Irish poet, novelist and nationalist Tom Kettle. He had earlier written, 'I have seen war and faced modern artillery and know what an outrage it is against simple men.'[52] Those in Ireland forgot this suffering. The division included newly raised battalions from all eight Irish infantry regiments at the time grouped into three brigades each soldier wore a shamrock on his back or arm. They went into the fight at the Somme and Messines in 1917 and were effectively destroyed on 21 March 1918 during the great German offensive of that year.[53]

Recruitment for the British Army after the Rising began to drop. There was frequent hostility in Ireland to British soldiers.[54] There was also growing distrust of Irish soldiers within the British Army as well as in Ireland. Soldiers of the 16th Irish Division returning to Ireland on leave met with incidents on the streets and women became increasingly reluctant to be seen with men in British uniform.[55] But at a different level there was discreet co-operation and support offered from serving British soldiers. According to David FitzPatrick, 'the young men who organised and drilled the Volunteer companies of 1917-1919 were by no means typical of the force as a whole. As in

[51]Ibid

[52]Ibid

[53]Ibid

[54]Bowen, p.245

[55]Deirdre McMahon, 'Ireland the Empire and the Commonwealth,' in Kevin Kenny, ed., *Ireland and the British Empire: Oxford history of the British Empire companion series,* p.203

1914, immense respect was accorded the relatively few people who knew how to clean a rifle and march in a straight line. Just as most pre-war companies had been trained by army reservists, so most post-Rising companies were helped by army deserters, soldiers on leave, or demobs.'[56]

Indeed the British government at the time was alarmed at the number of demobbed and unemployed ex-soldiers, who reacting to the strange conditions on the ground in Ireland, were finding it difficult to recondition themselves and as a result aligned themselves with various political factions. Many ex-soldiers had become estranged to their previous identities, loyalties and conditions when they returned from the war as a result of the changed political atmosphere while they were abroad. Some in the establishment believed that the 'great mass' of demobs had been so disgusted by the government's errors that 'they were ready to throw in their lot with the Republicans where they have not done so already.'[57] The number who did cannot be quantified, but again according to Fitzpatrick, in Clare 'the most efficient and reckless IRA fighting-men received their training in the Allied armies during the European War'.[58] Some were blatant in their actions, for instance at the Newbridge petty sessions in June 1917 an ex-sergeant of the Connaught Rangers was sentenced for two months for obstructing police. He was found in charge of eight boys while illegally drilling them.[59]

Others contributed in a more clandestine fashion and one such case is that of an army sergeant based in Dublin during 1916. At the outbreak of war Edward Hanley was serving with the 4th Battalion Dublin Fusiliers and during 1916 was back in Dublin on sick leave from France. He was store-man in Portobello Barracks, Rathmines and

[56]David FitzPatrick, *Politics in Irish life 1913-1921: provincial experience of war and revolution,* (2nd ed, Hampshire, 1993), p.202
[57]Ibid, p.203
[58]Ibid
[59]James Durney, p.40

while there the Irish Citizen Army asked him to acquire some weapons. Hanley relocated close to a hundred weapons over a period of a couple of years without being caught.[60] Soldiers also arranged to have their weapons bought and even stolen by Volunteers.[61] In 1917, Jimmy Mooney gave the first rifle procured by the Trim and Longwood companies of the IRA to them while he was home on leave from the front. He ran the risk of court-martial for returning without it, as would have been the case with all soldiers.[62]

At the same time and especially during the War of Independence in Meath and elsewhere, being a former member of the British Army was a dangerous matter. However, it has been pointed out that within the ranks of the Volunteers there were men who had seen service in previous British wars.[63] At the height of the War of Independence many Irishmen began to feel that the enemies that they had recently been asked to fight in the Great War, while wearing British uniforms, represented far less of a threat than those Englishmen of the crown forces who still laid claim to an ill-founded dominance of Ireland.[64]

Irish War of Independence and Ex-Servicemen

On 21 January 1919, the newly elected Sinn Féin members of the British House of Commons met in the Mansion House in Dublin, instituting the first Dáil Éireann. Refusing to go to the Westminster parliament and having formalised a parliament of their own, Robert Barton T.D. representing Kildare/Wicklow and a former British soldier read the English version of the 'Message to Free Nations'. The Irish elected representatives, having approved a general constitution confirmed the Proclamation read by Pearse at the GPO in 1916 and ratified the establishment of the Irish Republic pledging Dáil Éireann

[60]Edward Hanley, BMH, NAI, WS 635
[61]Ibid
[62]Oliver Coogan, *Politics and war in Meath 1913-23*, (Dublin, 1993), p.111
[63]Ibid, p.164
[64]Philip Orr, Field of bones: *an Irish division at Gallipoli* (Dublin, 2006), pp 209

and the people 'to make this declaration effective by every means at our command' and demanded 'the evacuation of our country by the British garrison'.[65] The Volunteer movement immediately recognised the Dáil as the legal government of Ireland. To make it possible for this new government to function the Volunteers were placed under the control of the Minister of Defence who took full responsibility for military actions. The Volunteers were from that time on known as the Irish Republican Army and each officer and volunteer now took an oath of allegiance to the government of the Irish Republic. Republican courts and a republican police force were set up to dispense and enforce republican justice.

During 1917 and 1918 the Volunteers had already began reorganising, spearheaded by 1916 survivors and released internees from the republican university "Frongoch" prison. By 1917 the Volunteer army had started to produce their own training manuals based on the British version.[66] At first there was no real policy to procure arms and what was later to develop into large-scale guerrilla warfare initially took the form of raids for arms. Like the company in Kells in Meath in 1917, the new recruits to the movement began securing weapons, learning the mechanisms and how to fire them, load and unload, bayonet practice and drilling their men on semaphore signalling.[67]

Ex-British soldiers came to the fore here too. Paddy Garret was one such ex-serviceman. A veteran of both the Boer War and World War I, he was sent from headquarters to organise the various companies in Meath, to instruct the men in the use of firearms and to supervise drilling.[68] Jack Hunt, who was awarded the Distinguished Service Order at Guinchy during the war in 1916 and later joined the IRA, did

---

[65]James Durney, p.47

[66]The Mulcahy papers contain four training manuals for weapons etc dating between 1917-1919, Mulcahy papers, UCDA, P7a/21,

[67]Coogan, p.92

[68]Ibid, p.106

the same.[69] The reorganised Irish Volunteer movement, according to Peter Hart, was both anti party and anti British.[70] The public reaction to the executions of 1916, as was already mentioned was a major factor in consolidating opposition to British rule. This combined with the frustration caused by the failure to implement Home Rule, dissent with the First World War and most of all, perhaps, the prospect of extension of conscription to Ireland aroused much ill feeling. After the success of Sinn Féin in the 1918 elections, and with the British content to ignore the moves to set up the Dáil the Irish government proclaimed

> *'that the existing state of war between Ireland and England can never be ended until Ireland is definitely evacuated by the armed forces of England'.* [71]

Though nominally under Sinn Féin control the various IRA units around the country had a great deal of autonomy in their local areas and this lack of control is seen as one of the reasons for the drift into hostilities against crown forces.

The Irish War of Independence began ominously on 21 January 1919 with the shooting of two RIC men in Tipperary, the same day the first Dáil met in Dublin, but the real war didn't begin for a while. There was a kind of phoney war in existence while both sides sized each other up; this gave the movement time to organise. Some in the Volunteer leadership saw the best way of forcing the British out would be through the formation of the military in a conventional style of establishment, such as brigades and battalion structures, that would fight decisive battles in fixed position.[72] However, this could never

---

[69]Deirdre McMahon, 'Ireland the Empire and the commonwealth,' in Kevin Kenny, ed., *Ireland and the British Empire: Oxford history of the British Empire companion series,* p.204

[70]Peter Hart, *The IRA and its enemies: violence and community in Cork 1916-1923* (New York, 1998), p.46

[71]M. L. R. Smith, *Fighting for Ireland: The military strategy of the Irish republican movement* (London, 1995), p.32

[72]De Valera believed in the idea but Mulcahy never really forgave him for pushing the concept of pitching the forces against each other that culminated in the attack on the Customs House, which turned into a military fiasco

have worked because of the vastly superior resources that the British could rely upon. The 1916 fighting capabilities and the later raid on the Customs House, pushed by de Valera, was evidence enough for that. These small sieges and desire for set piece battles were of importance as symbols but drained resources. So the nationalist military thinking reverted back and relied on a new strategy, which was based around the non-committal of resources to any hastily organised venture.

General Mulcahy, for one, did not believe in large-scale confrontations during the War of Independence although this changed in the Civil War. In 1919 Michael Brennan arranged a general onslaught on the RIC all over his East Clare brigade area for one night and had not informed GHQ. When Mulcahy found out, Brennan was chastised but carried on regardless.[73] A new tactical doctrine that argued for a move away from large-scale confrontations and towards more mobile forms of warfare using smaller military formations in combat was envisaged.[74] This meant that properly trained soldiers were needed as it involved getting in close and personal, which not all volunteers could stomach. Various contributions to the study of the IRA including those by Peter Hart (2003) and Sinead Joy (2005) raised the question as to whether its members in volatile areas such as Kerry and Cork really were the natural-born fighters depicted in nationalist and republican popular traditions.[75] In Kerry for example, volunteers would retreat from ideal ambush sites or get sick during the fight and lie down until the shooting was over.[76] These men had little or no combat experience. But during this period some like Tom Barry for example brought experience to the IRA. The discipline to conduct an ambush or be a part of a flying column may have been due in part to the experience of ex-soldiers.

[73]David Fitzpatrick, *Politics and Irish life 1913-1921* (Cork, 1998), p.186;
  Michael Brennan, The war in Clare 1911-1921 (Dublin, 1980), p.38
[74]Smith, p.35
[75]Peter Hart, *The IRA & its enemies;* Peter Hart, *The IRA at war* 1916-1923
  (New York, 2003); Sinead Joy, *The IRA in Kerry 1916-1921* (Cork, 2005), pp 94-95
[76]Joy, pp 94-96

Although others were quite successful without this background, success in the Irish War of Independence and Civil War may owe much more than is acknowledged to British military training and ex-soldiers and doctrine. These people had a different sense of discipline and organisation. The growing number of raids and activities undertaken by the IRA meant more exciting involvement for the rank and file and these operations helped expose volunteers who were more willing and daring than others. This may have been largely as a result of the tendency to rely on men with experience and probably accounts for large numbers of ex-soldiers among the IRA fighting forces.[77]

According to Florrie O'Donoghue 'hundreds of men with British Army service served loyally and well in the IRA, some of them being the foremost among the intrepid fighters.'[78] From a column man's point of view 'if you were not a column man, you were small fry, the whole of the rank and file were a good help, the inactive men stayed at home and the rest of the men were with the columns.'[79] This attitude caused many problems to occur between columns and companies.

Activists in Bandon, Fermoy and Kanturk recruited ex-soldiers for their military skills over strenuous local objections.[80] The flying column became the chief offensive weapon of the IRA.[81] The column was supplied with the bulk of the arms available from brigades. According to Florence O'Donoghue 'there was sufficient supply of rifles to arm small columns and those on whole-time service could better defend themselves as organised groups than as individuals'.[82]

[77] Joost Augusteijn, *From public defiance to guerrilla warfare: the experience of ordinary volunteers in the Irish War of Independence 1916- 1921* (Dublin, 1996), p.97

[78] Florence O' Donoghue, *No other law* (Dublin, 1954), p.145

[79] O' Malley papers UCDA, P17/b/124, 123

[80] Ibid

[81] Robert Kee, *The green flag: ourselves alone* (London, 1972), iii, p.114

[82] Florence O' Donoghue, 'Guerrilla warfare in Ireland 1919-1921, in *An Cosantoir* (May, 1963), no.1, p.298

Another advantage of small committed units was that they had the time to train and develop skills, which benefited the movement as a whole. The small columns were far better suited to fighting a war than the vast cumbersome Volunteer organisation. They had virtually all the rifles in the brigade; time enough for training and the incentive to develop military skills.[83] This happened for example in much the same way that military advisors and experts are sent abroad by modern governments to train emerging military type factions and other underground groups for insurgency and campaigns to undermine established regimes. These operations are quite successful in militarising recruits, just like the ex-British servicemen impacted on the evolution of the IRA and National Army in the same fashion. As with those modern experts it only takes a few to enlighten and professionalise the many in a short period of time. Those men, trained in the handling of weapons, and the men who led them under the stress of battle were able to galvanise those they sought to influence in the fundamentals of combat and the art of war.

In the case of the early Volunteers and IRA there was much more than a few, indeed there were many. If their influence meant, that as a result of the training they provided those being so trained could manoeuvre in tactical formations, while armed, across uneven and broken terrain without accidentally shooting or inflicting casualties on themselves or their comrades, or otherwise compromise their positions, then it meant that they were becoming skilled combatants. This was by no means an easy task to achieve. Ernie O'Malley described a column training camp and instructors mentioning the input of Captain Prout, an ex-American officer, who had been attached to the intelligence squad and who later took the pro-Treaty side during the Civil War and also Dermot McManus, an ex-British officer who was attached to the training staff at GHQ. 'Volunteers were trained first for two weeks in the application of arms.'[84]

---

[83]Fitzpatrick, p.181

[84]Mulcahy papers contain seven *Oglaigh na hEireann* training manuals produced between 1919-1921, Mulcahy papers, UCDA, P7a/23

By the end of the period they had the elementary training of an infantry soldier. During parades the ceremony was a mixture of American and British drill.'[85] O'Malley's brother had fought with the Royal Dublin Fusiliers in the war and he himself had a great fascination with military manuals, and had originally planned to join the British Army. The events of 1916 drastically altered his direction.[86]

With the British committed to a military solution with part of their agenda coming through the reprisal tactics of other ex-British soldiers, i.e. the Auxiliaries and Black and Tans (the IRA was guilty of this too) people on the Republican side did their best to combat them. Tom Barry had been a young soldier in the Great War.[87] He was one of many Catholic ex-servicemen who found military or paramilitary employment under a nationalist flag despite the hostility that their war service had provoked.[88]

Barry was commander of the West Cork Flying Column and he later explained his change of allegiance in terms of spiritual conversion. Whereas he had joined the British Army in 1915 to 'see what war was like, to get a gun, to see new countries and to feel a grown man, his subsequent enrolment in the Irish Volunteers resulted from him being awakened to his Irish nationalism by news of the Easter Rising whilst serving in Mesopotamia.'[89] This is interesting as it contrasts with the feelings of other Irishmen serving in the British Army at the time, such as Tom Kettle, who before he was killed felt bewildered and betrayed. But even those who were non-aligned during the war returned to Ireland and took sides.

---

[85]Ernie O' Malley, *The singing flame* (2nd ed., Dublin, 1978), pp 20-22
[86]Deirdre McMahon, 'Ireland, the Empire and the Commonwealth,' in Kevin Kenny, ed., *Ireland and the British Empire: Oxford history of the British Empire companion series*, (Oxford, 2004), p.204
[87]Tom Barry, officer commanding Cork no. 2 brigade flying column 1920 –21, Commandant General IRA 1921, BMH, NAI, WS 1754
[88]David Fitzpatrick, 'Militarism in Ireland 1900-1922, in Thomas Bartlett and Keith Jeffery (eds.) *A military history of Ireland,* p.400
[89]Ibid

Tom Garvin describes the ex-servicemen and their militarist nature by saying:

'IRA leaders tended to be younger during the War of Independence, which was a general shift in the movement away from the IRB. Many of them had not had any direct involvement with extreme nationalist politics and many had sympathised with the Irish party. Many had had experience in the British Army in World War I. In some ways they were not unlike other members of their generation who had attempted to remain in army life at the end of the war by joining paramilitary associations. In a sense they were not unlike many of the young men in the British forces who had become militarised by the war and who had "contempt for politics", "distrust for civilian leadership" and a "warrior mystique". The distrust was combined with a rebellion against the older generation as being effete, corrupt, un-heroic and above all civilian.'[90]

Barry had returned to Ireland in February 1919 becoming an IRA intelligence and training officer for the West Cork Brigade by May 1920. Although there were other column leaders who had been successful without the background of British military training it was Barry who later became a legendary figure by displaying his experience in the Kilmichael ambush with his West Cork Flying Column. On 28 November 1920, they wiped out two lorry loads of Auxiliaries on the Macroom to Dunmanway road at a cost of three dead.[91] He held his men in a disciplined ambush close to the road allowing only for attack and not retreat.[92] A grenade and rifle attack was followed by hand to hand fighting after which eighteen rifles and 180 rounds of ammunition were captured, including thirty revolvers and some grenades. Barry's men had gone thirty hours without food. They had marched twenty-six miles and had lain soaked and frozen on exposed rocks waiting in ambush. To remind them that they were

---

[90]Tom Garvin, *The evolution of nationalist politics,* pp 142-147
[91]Duggan, p.48
[92]Hart, *The IRA and its enemies,* pp 32-33

soldiers who could not afford to wallow in the luxury of shock Barry drilled them severely amidst the dead immediately after the action, or as Peter Hart concludes, the killing of prisoners and wounded men. The Auxiliaries lost seventeen dead.

This event has fuelled much debate in recent times with Meda Ryan defending Barry's actions against the theories of Peter Hart. However, the Auxiliary's superman image had been dented. The discipline that Barry had instilled in his men brought a new edge to the fighting although Peter Hart sees Barry's role differently and explains that on his order British servicemen were cut down after they had surrendered. Later Barry became controversial for many things: he led an outstanding attack against a large column of crown forces on 19 March 1921, inflicting heavy losses and he ordered the shooting on sight of troops from the Essex Regiment. He became Deputy Commandant and Training Officer of the 1st Southern Division IRA before resigning in September 1921. He took the anti-Treaty side and was captured by the National Army at the beginning of the Civil War as they feared his influence, but he escaped to play an important role, later becoming IRA Chief of Staff.

Issues for ex-servicemen

This use of ex-soldiers by the IRA is in contrast to attitudes towards these men in 1919, which saw their return en masse from the war. Many soldiers arrived home damaged both physically and mentally. Some were weary, sick of the violence and destruction and some even hated the British Army. They had witnessed social segregation within the army and hated the British officer and his class. There had been official and many unofficial executions of Irish soldiers during the war.

---

[93]Meda Ryan, 'Tom Barry and the Kilmichael Ambush, in *History Ireland,* vol. 13 no. 5 (2005), pp 14-18; Meda Ryan, *Tom Barry Freedom fighter* (Cork, 2003), pp 18-22, 31-38
[94]Ibid
[95]Hart, *The IRA and its enemies,* pp 22-26
[96]Padraic O' Farrell, *Who's who in the Irish War of Independence and Civil War 1916-1923,* (Dublin, 1997), p.6

British officers ordered the executions of men mentally scarred and disturbed for desertion and cowardice when what they should have received was sympathy and help. They had witnessed the suicides of their comrades who had had enough of the rats, the lice, the living conditions and the boredom but most of all the years of attrition.

They came back hating the system but they had helped win the war and should have been received as heroes. Some were given cottages and smallholdings, 46 per cent of Irish ex-servicemen were drawing the out of work donations in November of that year.[97] Local boards and county councils all over Munster for example passed resolutions not to employ ex-soldiers.[98] By October 1919, thirty five thousand ex-service men were receiving the "out of work donation" in Ireland, an unemployment ratio of 46 per cent compared with only 10 per cent in Britain. In mid-January 1921, approximately 24,000 veterans were listed on the "live register" in Ireland. In Cork more than 4,500 ex-servicemen were unemployed, representing about half of all the recorded wartime enlistment.[99] Many were institutionalised and returned to the comradeship of the army. Many of these soldiers had been members at one stage of the original Irish Volunteers. They went to France with the National Volunteers as their way of securing independence and serving Ireland. Is it any wonder men joined the Republican movement?

However, the returning veterans were not, as a whole, accepted into the ranks of the IRA, nor were they wholly accepted back into society. They were threatened and boycotted, their houses burnt and the GAA refused them permission to rejoin clubs.[100] The legendary Tom Barry,

---

[97]Hart, *The IRA and its enemies*, p.312.

[98]Ibid.

[99]Ireland and the war: - Early remembrance and revival, 4eremdw.html

[100]Jane Leonard, 'Facing the finger of scorn: veterans memories of Ireland after the Great War', in Martin Evans and Ken Lunn (eds.) *War and memory in the twentieth century* (Oxford, 1997), pp 59-73; Donal Hall, 'World War I and nationalist politics in Louth 1914-1920, in *Maynooth series in local history* (Dublin, 2005), p.47

in the beginning, was under constant suspicion, even while a member of the Republican movement and while training volunteers.[101] But it is interesting that the Cork IRA, according to Florence O'Donoghue, had hundreds of active ex-servicemen in its ranks and used them and reservists to train the volunteers.[102] Men like Captain McCarthy an ex-Royal Electrical Mechanical Engineer of the British Army and an explosives expert who assisted the West Cork Flying Column after the action at Crossbarry and prepared the mine used at Rosscarbery on 30 March 1921.[103] Also Peter Monahan of Bandon, a Scottish soldier of Irish parents who had served in the Cameron Regiment in Cork after the Great War. He deserted in 1920 and also joined the West Cork Brigade assisting with explosives and taking part in most of its major operations. He was killed in action at Crossbarry on 19 March 1921.[104] These men and many like them were not afraid to kill members of the British military even though they had once worn the same uniform and previously been a part of the comrade fold.

The active service veterans of the British army included James Coleman, Sean Healy, Con Conroy, Pat Margetts and Eugene O'Connell. Sean Murray, the brigade training officer and primary organiser of the brigade's flying column was a former Irish Guard who saw action in Flanders. The brigade chaplain Father Dominic O'Connor had served in Salonica in Greece and Tom Barry had served in Mesopotamia, now modern Iraq. While the IRA was a tight organisation that did not seek out new recruits after hostilities commenced in 1920, it never prohibited ex-servicemen from joining its ranks.[105] Ignatius O' Neill of Milltown Malbay in Co. Clare and an ex-soldier of the Irish Guards led the 4th Battalion of the Mid-Clare

---

[101]Hart, *The IRA and its enemies*, p.148
[102]O'Donoghue, *No other law*, pp 145 & 73
[103]Padraig O' Farrell, p.58
[104]Ibid, p.70
[105]John Borgonovo, *Spies, informers and the anti-Sinn Fein society, the intelligence war in Cork city 1920-1921* (Dublin, 2007), pp 81-2

Brigade during the Rineen Ambush on 20 September 1920, which killed three British soldiers.[106] John Coates of Spancel Hill, near Ennis, was another. Described as an itinerant tailor he had been acquitted of carrying arms but found to be a deserter from the Machine Gun Corps (MGG) '. . . his tailoring was only a cloak, in reality he was a machine-gun instructor to the Clare IRA.'[107]

The Irish War of Independence and Civil War certainly had sectarian dimensions. During the War of Independence period Protestants made up 8 percent of the population in County Cork but constituted 36 percent of those shot by the IRA and owned seventy five percent of the houses burnt by them also.[108] This sectarian agenda by the IRA also stretched to ex-servicemen on a countrywide scale as a result of their background and what they were thought to represent.

On 5 July 1920, the body of an ex-soldier who had fought at Gallipoli in 1915 was taken from the River Boyne near Kilmessan. It had been tied down with a pair of axles.[109] Nicholas Prendergast, a former British Army Captain and ex-Christian Brother was drowned by the Black and Tans at Fermoy in Cork in December.[110] In November of the same year a report was sent to Dublin Castle on the kidnapping of Daniel Lynch aged 25 an ex-soldier who had been taken from his home at Kilpatrick, in Kilshannen on 5th November by armed and masked men.[111] These were some examples of the incidents occurring in a spiral of violence

---

[106]Padraig O'Farrell, p.83

[107]Weekly Intelligence Summary G/18/89/1/2 copy no 43 for the 6th Division signed by its commander Major General E.P. Strickland on 17/5/21and reproduced in O'Donoghue, *No other law,* p.325 appendix

[108]Sean Sexton, A proper perspective-a review of Henry Patterson's 'Ireland since 1939: the persistence of conflict,' in *Magill: Irelands political and cultural monthly,* October, 2006, p.27

[109]Coogan, p.167

[110]O'Farrell, p.88

[111]Dublin castle report dated 12 November 1920 under the title 'Public control and administration 1884-1921, CO 904, (AS41.5 CO904 Box 168 Reel 091)

towards ex-servicemen. Jane Leonard estimates that between 1919 and 1924 approximately 120 ex-servicemen were murdered. Some were spies and shot as such but the majority were innocent and killed as retrospective punishment for their service in the Great War.[112]

On the 4 May 1921, during the height of its attrition, Liam Lynch wrote to Mulcahy at GHQ suggesting that in the future the IRA should shoot a local loyalist for each Volunteer shot in British custody and although this was probably designed to prevent the enemy from shooting prisoners it may have been one of those scenarios that made it easier to victimise ex-soldiers.[113] Demobilised servicemen and their families had already become targets for abuse soon after the Easter Rising. By July that year they were fighting 'Sinn Féiners' in the streets of Cork City and other towns. After one incident an ex-soldier was beaten and derided 'as another rejected soldier who sold his country for a Saxon shilling'. He told a reporter 'it is just because I am a soldier. I am in dread of living in my own town'.

Another woman declared 'that a soldier's wife would be murdered in the town by the people'.[114] Republicans saw the recruitment for the British and later the National Army as being almost 'entirely drawn' from the ranks of the undeserving poor: all scruff and corner boys. Ex-soldiers returning from the war were tarred with the same brush. These men along with their wives and mothers — 'shawlies' and 'separation women'- were classed as drunken rabble, and subjected to withering Republican scorn.[115]

---

[112]Leonard, p.47

[113]Valiulis, pp 68-72

[114]*The Irish Times*, 20 July. 1916; *The Irish Times*, 5 August. 1916; Hart, *The IRA and its enemies*, p.311

[115]O'Malley papers, UCDA P17a/34; Hart, *The IRA and its enemies*, p.149

According to Tom Garvin:

> *'much of the opposition to conscription in Ireland during the war was class derived . . . the greatest resistance to conscription reportedly came originally from the "farming and commercial classes" because educated Catholics were likely to have to serve in the ranks. This was particularly so in the early months of the war as commissions were usually reserved for the public school alumni. Fear of proletarianisation, rather than either cowardice or nationalism, prompted resistance'*[116]

What about Josie Faulkner, an ex-British Soldier arrested with a comrade for a shooting on the Shankill golf course in Co. Dublin on the orders of his IRA commanders? He was almost beaten to death by the RIC, court-martialled and given ten years and as a result lost his pension for his service in the Great War.[117] During the Meath Hunt Steeplechase on Thursday 7 April 1920 in Navan Co. Meath, an attempt was made on the life of an RIC sergeant. The man was arrested and given fifteen years penal servitude (one of the longest imposed) for the shooting. He was an ex-British soldier who had been decorated for bravery during the war.[118] Were he and Faulkner some of those "corner boy" types? Were the ex-soldiers who served the IRA considered in this way?

The ex-servicemen who now found themselves in the IRA received no pay or recognition and most of all, like their Volunteer comrades, no protection under international laws of warfare like the Geneva Convention. Obviously some ex-soldiers in the IRA during the War of Independence had a paradoxical existence when claiming their British Army pensions and at the same time fighting against the police and military forces of the crown. These men had, at some level, earned the trust of their Republican comrades. Other ex-soldiers, many

---

[116]Garvin, *Nationalist revolutionaries in Ireland,* p.168
[117]James MacSweeney, The fight in the Bray area', in *Dublin's fighting story,* pp 191-192
[118]Coogan, p.170

completely innocent and non-aligned, suffered intimidation and death at the hands of Republicans, as a result of their propaganda, a paradox of the period.

There had always been resentment and intolerance within republican circles towards Irishmen who had joined the British Army even prior to the Great War. There was also little condemnation of shootings and intimidation of members of the police and military forces and ex-servicemen, and as we have seen and shall see later this carried on throughout the period to the Civil War and after.[119] The IRA justified these tactics employed against Irish veterans, by the republican movement, at the time because their existence in the community was seen to undermine the revolution's effectiveness as many refused to join Sinn Féin or recognise its legitimacy. British military commanders and politicians also saw these veterans as strategic pawns in the campaign to undermine republican extremism.

John Borgovo's excellent study of the Cork IRA's intelligence war contradicts the theories of both Jane Leonard and Peter Hart in that he says there is little evidence to support a concerted policy against ex-servicemen or to purge them from a New Ireland. He proposed that the vast numbers of ex-servicemen in Cork city could be found in all walks of life some of whom who were intimate with local IRA volunteers but not involved. However a disproportionate number of the men they shot as spies were ex-servicemen.

'Almost all were working class with modest standing in the community…no close connections or blood between them and any Cork Volunteers…a number were impoverished veterans struggling to integrate themselves into the community… faced with numerous cases of local complicity within the crown forces, the city's IRA leadership probably found it easiest to assassinate isolated men of low social standing, rather than prominent pillars of the community, close associates or members of republican families'[120]

---

[119]The Mulcahy papers contain draft orders concerning attacks on enemy NCOs and families of members of the RIC, Mulcahy papers, UCDA P7/A/19
[120]Borgovono, pp 66-98

After the National Volunteers returned from the Great War some of them became the most effective guerrilla fighters and officers of the Irish Volunteers and IRA.[121] Others with less notoriety contributed to the military struggle with many coming from non-Irish regiments of the British Army. For instance there is the example of Company Sergeant Martin Doyle who had been awarded the Victoria Cross for destroying the crew of a German gun emplacement 'single-handed' with his rifle and bayonet in September 1918. Less than a year later, Doyle was a member of the IRA. Owen Nolan, from Limerick, served with the Royal Horse Artillery. He was wounded and later joined the IRA. He was the last man to surrender to Free State troops at William St RIC barracks during the Civil War and was interned with Sean T. O'Kelly.[122]

Private Jim Fitzgerald from Graiguenamanagh in Co. Kilkenny was one of those quiet men from a military background whose impact on the IRA was subtle but effective. Born in 1881, he joined the 3rd battalion Royal Irish Regiment of the British Army at the age of twenty-four in Kilkenny from his family home in Tinnahinch. His military service included the whole of the Great War from 1915 onwards with a great portion of his experience gained in the Balkans campaigns.

During this time he was wounded in the neck by shrapnel from the explosion of an enemy artillery shell. After the war he returned home and joined the local IRA unit were he helped to train its members in weapons handling and other military matters. He also covertly ferried weapons on the local canal, a considerable asset of his civilian employment on the barges. During the period of the Irish War of Independence the Fitzgerald family home was raided on numerous occasions by crown forces. Although from a republican background Jim never took a combatant side in the Irish Civil War but it is very

---

interesting indeed that future generations of his family, including his grandson Jim and a number of his great-grandsons, would later join the Irish Defence Forces, giving a combined total of around seventy years service. This service included numerous United Nations peacekeeping missions to various trouble spots around the world including the Congo, Cyprus, Lebanon, Liberia and the Balkans.[123]

Michael Grace who was related to Jim Fitzgerald and who was also from the Tinnahinch area was a stretcher-bearer in the Great War with the Royal Army Medical Corps (RAMC) and was known throughout his life as "Doc" as a result of his wartime experience. He would recount in later life how he swept the littered battlefields after major actions looking for casualties, he would have to 'decide who would live or die amongst the injured'. Because of his limited resources, his best efforts could only scratch the surface. He received a bravery award, which hung in the family home for many years. Later after stealing some alcohol from the Officers' Mess with a number of friends and on being threatened with courts-martial and execution he told the investigating officer that the plan had been his alone and that he alone should be executed. His life was spared and after the war he too joined the local IRA unit and trained them in the use of firearms.

An incident that has been handed down through his family history recounts the day that while he was instructing the local IRA in their drill hall on the proper loading and unloading of a snub nosed revolver, he accidentally discharged a round through the ceiling of the room. This instantly caused the panicked evacuation of his students as the loud and echoed report of the gunfire would certainly herald the arrival of the dreaded Black and Tans.

---

[123]I am extremely grateful to Mr Jim Hayles for recounting the Hayles, Fitzgerald and Grace family history and Tinnahinch histories to me. Jim Hayles is the grandson of Jim Fitzgerald and has himself had long service in the Irish army, as indeed do his sons. Mr Hayles also had English family members involved in the Great War

On another occasion Mr. Grace's brother-in-law Jack Conran, a wounded ex-soldier, made an innocent approach to some British soldiers outside a pub. This almost led to his arbitrary execution by one of their members. He was about to start a conversation with a soldier as old soldiers often do, when a 'Tan' cocked his revolver and put it to Jack's head and was about to pull the trigger when the distressed screams of his wife attracted the attention of an officer. The officer on hearing of the British Army connection put an end to the altercation.[124] In many cases the ex-British service of IRA volunteers was detrimental to their continued survival while in the custody of the crown forces but in some cases it helped.

According to David Fitzpatrick, veterans who changed allegiance found no inconsistency in reapplying their obedience and skill to new masters. They relished the military life but cared little for the contending rhetoric of patriotism.[125] Irishmen had long been a part of the tradition of military service in the British Army despite the ambivalent relationship between the two nations. Throughout the early struggle for independence the training of volunteers in the basic military skills was conducted in a covert if hazardous fashion, geared solely towards meeting the immediate requirements for sporadic encounters with enemy forces. Post war development of the Irish Volunteers owed more to the British Army than a mere infusion of sympathetic ex-service men. From its foundation the force had followed British Army practice in its organisation and training.'[126] As their primary function shifted from display towards combat the Volunteers moved beyond a peacetime militia on parade to the grim practicality of an army of war.[127] This practice and the abhorrence of the use of ex-soldiers would come into greater effect with the reorganisation of the army during the Irish Civil War.

---

[124]Ibid, Michael Grace was Grand-Uncle to Jim Hayles
[125]Bartlett and Jeffery, p.400
[126]Mulcahy papers, UCDA, P7/A/26-33
[127]Bartlett and Jeffery, p.402

Major General McSweeney, Director Military Aviation and Colonel C. F. Russell, Director of Civil Aviation 1922 (both ex RAF) *Courtesy of the Irish Air Corps.*

OGLAIG NA h-EIREANN.

VOLUNTEER RESERVE

Voluntary Levy, July, 1922.

PUBLIC NOTICE.

In order to complete the quota of the undermentioned Brigade, Recruiting for the Volunteer Reserve has been resumed at the following addresses:—

No. 3 Charlemont Terrace, Dun Laoghaire
Tallaght (Aerodrome) Camp, Tallaght
Greystones Coastguard Station
Church Street Barracks, Wicklow
Avondale House, Rathdrum
Arklow Coastguard Station

As only a limited number of recruits are required to complete the quota, those desirous of joining should report at once at one of the above Recruiting Stations.

Terms of Service.

Pay:—Two Shillings and Sixpence per day and all found. Dependents' Allowance to Married men in accordance with the circumstances of each case.

Recruits will proceed immediately after enrolment to a Training and Equipping Depot, where they will receive Uniform, Equipment, Rifle and Ammunition, and undergo a short course of Training. They will then be available for active service in the Brigade Area or elsewhere for a **Period of Six Months,** after which they will return to their Homes and Civilian Occupations. Having so returned they will be liable to Weekly Parades (in the same way as hitherto with Volunteer Companies), and will form a Reserve to be called up for Active Service in case of National Emergency.

(Signed) **NIALL MAC NEILL,** Brigadier,

Commanding No. 2 Brigade, 2nd Eastern Division.

Harbour Barracks, Dun Laoghaire, Co. Dublin.

Call up for Volunteer Reserve, July 1922. *Irish Independent.*

Young armed soldier. *Courtesy of the National Library of Ireland.*

Michael Collins *(second left)* and Emmet D'alton *(centre).*
Courtesy of Irish Military Archives.

Some Lancs at Tallaght Camp. *South Dublin Local Studies Collection.*

"Big Fella" escape plane, a Martynside type A Mk II.
Courtesy of the Irish Air Corps.

Communications on this subject
uld be addressed to—

UNDER SECRETARY OF STATE,
COLONIAL OFFICE,
      LONDON, S.W.1,

l the following
umber quoted : 49041/22

Downing Street,

28 November, 1922.

Sir,

      I am directed by the Duke of Devonshire to request you to inform the Provisional Government that the Lords Commissioners of the Admiralty have brought to his notice the position of Naval Pensioners and Members of the various Naval Reserves resident in Southern Ireland w enlist in the Irish National Forces.

      2.   Their Lordships have no objection to such men accepting employment in the Forces of the Provisional Government provided that it is understood that in the event of a Naval mobilisation the Imperial Government would have a prior claim on their services. I am accordingly to enquire whether the Provisional Government are prepared to recognise the priority of such a claim.

           I am, Sir,
              Your obedient Servant

ECRETARY

ROVISIONAL GOVERNMENT OF IRELAND.

Letter from the Duke of Devonsire in relation to Naval personnel accepting employment in the Irish National Forces. *Courtesy of National Archives.*

> We but war when war
> Serves Liberty and Justice, Love and Peace
> Who said that such an emprise could be vain?
> Were they not one with Christ who strove and died?
> Let Ireland weep but not for sorrow. Weep
> That by her sons a land is sanctified
>
> Francis Ledwidge

Chapter III

CIVIL WAR 1922-1923

Faith, Honour and Allegiance

'No responsible spokesman for Sinn Fein ever suggested that because there was a political landslide, then later after the time when the then representatives of the Irish people advocated such cause of Irishmen going to join the British Army at the beginning of the war, that those who went to that war, believing it to be the best for serving their country should be stigmatised'[128]

Minister Kevin O'Higgins on the appointment of General W.R.E. Murphy as Chief Commissioner of the Dublin Metropolitan Police.

Reorganisation and ex-British soldiers

Machiavelli wrote 'The first way to lose your state is to neglect the art of war.' This was something that the new government in Ireland was to learn the hard way. During a private session of the Treaty debates Commandant Sean McKeown of the pro-Treaty side stated:

---

[128]*The Irish Times,* 7 May. 1923

'we are told by the minister of defence that the army is in a much stronger position, infinitely stronger now than it was before the Truce- well it may be. It may be stronger in some points-in point of members it is a bit stronger-in training it is a bit stronger...I know perfectly well I have charge of four thousand men. I do not here hesitate to say that number. But of that four thousand I have a rifle for every fifty. Now that is the position as far as I am concerned and I may add there is about as much ammunition as would last them about fifty minutes for that rifle. Now people talk lightly of when we are going to war. I hold they do not know a damn thing about it' [129]

The outcome of the Irish War of Independence was that the British withdrew, leaving Irish military and political forces in possession of the field. There had been a truce, which was signed in the Round Room of the Mansion House in Dublin by representatives of both armies. This brought hostilities to an end with effect from 11 July 1921. The Treaty was signed on 6 December and on 14 January 1922 the Provisional Government was brought into existence to administer the Free State of Southern Ireland, minus the six Northern counties as delineated. The Treaty gave Ireland the same constitutional status within the British Empire as that of Canada, New Zealand, the Commonwealth of Australia and the Union of South Africa. The Free State was to allow the facilities of harbours to British forces at request. Many prominent republicans and anti-Treaty personalities protested at this saying that this meant Ireland would remain under permanent British military occupation. The Treaty also provided for a boundary commission if the Northern Ireland parliament refused to join the Free State and that the new state would have full fiscal autonomy. The oath, which turned out to be one of the most contentious parts of the agreement, especially regarding the army, was to be taken by members of the Free State parliament, it read as follows:

I ... do solemnly swear true faith and allegiance to the constitution of the Irish Free State as by law established and that I will be

---

[129]Helen Litton, *The Irish Civil War: an illustrated history* (4th ed. Dublin, 2006), p.142

faithful to H.M. King George V, his heirs and successors by law in virtue of the common citizenship of Ireland with Great Britain and her adherence to and membership of the group of nations forming the British Commonwealth of Nations.

The terms of the Treaty came together under a document titled 'Articles of Agreement for a truce between Great Britain and Ireland'. What was unique and what was also lost on many at the time was that this document actually recognised Irish sovereignty. But it was not to be accepted universally. British troops began to evacuate the country and the British Commander in Ireland, General Neville Macready and General Emmet Dalton, National Army liaison officer, arranged the handing over of military installations and posts. Military problems became exceptionally difficult from this point and the army sometimes had to rush to take over vacated military posts before IRA units, they weren't always successful.

Those concerned with the inevitable economic repercussions of barrack closures (especially on the local business communities) contacted Dalton outlining their worries. But there were more pressing worries.[130] There would also be no foreign or homegrown investment or economic growth without a legal military to protect the constitution and state integrity. The police forces were disbanded and the resources of government transferred to Irish control.

However, the British administration was in ruins and its successor not yet established. As a result no police force or judicial system was functioning, the economy was at a standstill in the absence of security unemployment was rapidly increasing and many people were dissatisfied with the terms of the Treaty. The old aspirations and ideals of a republic remained, but as Patrick Long points out, 'a gradualist approach to the republic, via the Treaty and the dominion status it offered, was not going to be accepted without some resistance'.[131]

---

[130]Patrick Long, 'Organisation and development of the pro-Treaty forces, 1922-1924' in *The Irish sword: the journal of the military history society of Ireland,* Vol. XX, No. 82 (Dublin, 1997), p.309

[131]Patrick Long, p.309

Recognition of the Irish Republic was central to the Treaty debates, not least for those who were in opposition. They believed that the national sovereignty of the state and the historic unity of the country were in jeopardy of being surrendered at the threat of force from Britain. They wanted a republic and a complete break with the king and commonwealth. Liam Mellows declared that 'this Free State derives no authority from the Dáil. It derives authority solely from the British Government . . . we are undermining the Republic.'[132]

The Volunteer dynamic was about to change with a split in the army. Convincing the IRA of the army's continuing republican ideals was never fully achieved. Even a dynamic statement in the Dáil on 10 January 1922 by General Mulcahy that 'the army will remain the army of the Republic' never had the desired effect.[133] The government was extremely worried as there was said to be 114,652 soldiers still within the Volunteers or IRA, most without a function.[134] Added to this was a feeling of social upheaval and what's more the British were about to threaten re-occupation but in the end it was the worst type of scenario, Civil War. It would be fought by the IRA who, as de Valera put it on St. Patrick's Day at Thurles 'might have to wade through Irish blood, through the blood of soldiers of the Irish government and through perhaps the blood of some of the members of the government in order to get Irish freedom.'[135]

Supporters say the speech was meant as a warning but critics, with some justification, condemned it as incitement, which in the end turned out to be pretty accurate. The IRA was to base its opposition on the nature of the Treaty stating that 'it was approved in London by the Dáil under threat of war' and that 'it is only the Army of the Republic which can save the country from being forced – by the connivance of Mr Griffith and Mr Collins — to yield up its liberty under fear of war.'[136]

---

[132]Brian P. Murphy, 'The Irish Civil War 1922-1923: an anti-Treaty perspective', in *The Civil War 1922-23 special edition of the Irish sword the journal of the military history society of Ireland,* Vol. XX No.82 (Dublin, 1997), p.294
[133]Dail Debates, 10 January 1922
[134]Captain J. Sheehan, *Defence Forces handbook (Dublin, 1983),* pp 5-7
[135]Brian Murphy, p.295
[136]Ibid, p.296

Churchill had indeed threatened armed intervention in support of the Treaty by sending war materials and by early February was ready to commit troops, later deciding to leave British soldiers remaining in Ireland 'until we know the Irish people are going to stand by the Treaty.'[137]

The first indication of a serious threat of Civil War was the army convention, held in the Mansion House on 26 March 1922. Although General Mulcahy had prohibited it, 220 anti-Treaty delegates from forty-nine brigades turned up and spokesman for the convention, Rory O'Connor repudiated the authority of Dáil Éireann. Collins and de Valera tried to prevent hostilities by designing a pact that would bring together both sides in the army split through the rigging of elections for the third Dáil.

The Pact had also caused uproar in the British cabinet and in the Northern government. Although the Treaty offered a great deal more autonomy than was generally appreciated at the time, those opposed to it, as has already been pointed out, wanted a complete break with the King and commonwealth and desired the setting up of the longed for republic. The Treaty offer of independence limited this in several ways. The Free State would have the same status within the empire as Canada with a governor-general representing the King and British military forces still had claim to certain Irish ports.

Members of the Dáil would have to swear allegiance to the constitution of the Irish Free State in the first instance and to the King. This was not the republic the anti-Treaty-ites expected and the territorial integrity of the country was nullified with the fate of the North. Many anti-Treaty-ites spoke of betrayal of the pure and exalted ideals of the 1916 Proclamation and the Republic. The stage had been set for a war between former comrades and it would be fought with forces that were considered to be not entirely loyal on either side.

---

[137]Ibid, p.297

After the army split, General Dalton began organising the new force, which encompassed special emphasis and recommendations on the structure of GHQ and the Divisions by the time of the re-organisation of 1923.[138] He used a model, produced by a British officer named Down, which had been proven in the British system and was reflected very closely in the Irish model as early as July 1922.[139] It was this reorganisation, which began the Irish Army's difficult transition from a guerrilla force to a regular conventional style military entity during the Civil War conflict.

The Provisional Government had initially wanted to control the number of ex-British servicemen employed in the new Irish army for obvious reasons but they also knew the army needed them. The Commander in Chief reported in August 1922, that a 'limited number of ex-British officers had been taken into the army, that these were Irishmen and were employed mainly in an instructing capacity and in some cases in an assisting capacity.[140] The number of ex-servicemen was always greater than that which was officially portrayed. Dalton would have known the British disciplinary code and understood the effect it would have in helping to professionalise the army in Ireland when it was introduced. It was another way of moving away from the fraternity and familiarity between ranks in the guerrilla army model. So ex-servicemen had an important role from the beginning and they would have settled into a very familiar British system at most levels, even if the organisation operated in a very 'ad hoc' Irish fashion during the war. This ad hoc fashion meant that those from the other extreme found it possible to adapt to the new environment. Although the National Army would later use German, French and American influences including personnel, it is a fact that during the Irish revolution of 1913-1923 both the IRA and government forces realised the importance of trained professional soldiers and complied by using ex-British servicemen as a viable military asset, very effectively, throughout the period.

---

[138]Patrick Long, pp 315-6

[139]Ibid

[140]Discussion by Provisional Government of Ireland on employment of ex-British officers in raising of volunteer army 1922, NAI, Dept of Taoiseach papers, S1302

Alvin Jackson points out that Kevin O'Higgins, was extremely critical of the National Army during and after the Civil War when he was a government minister. O'Higgins had a brother killed in Europe during World War I, and although he fought the separatist war against the British in Ireland he later became comfortably accommodated within Britain's Irish dominion model in the 1920s.[141] Many of the old civil service administrators too had simply changed employer and allegiances and began to build the infrastructure under the new Free State. Captain G.H. Mew, R.E. (Royal Engineers) was appointed the first head of the Ordnance Survey in Ireland on 1st April 1922, when the Dublin office of the twenty-six counties, together with a small compliment of staff, was handed over to the Provisional Government and placed under the Department of Land and Agriculture and later the Department of Finance.[142]

The old civil servants and administrative officers already had the skills and began to make an impact but what about the impact of ex-British soldiers on the Irish Army and their experiences during Ireland's Civil War period? The Provisional Government was totally dependent on the army but had no confidence in its ability or potential performance prior to or during the early months of the Civil War. Sean McMahon, the army's quartermaster and later to be a chief of staff, described how it was only after the fighting in Dublin that the realisation came to them that they were in for a long struggle and they began looking around for an army.[143] GHQ at Beggars Bush barracks had originally thought that an army consisting of a 'Voluntary Levy' or the 'Government Reserve Scheme' could produce a combined regular and reserve force of 30,000

[141]Alvin Jackson, Ireland, 'the union and the Empire 1800-1960', in Kevin Kenny, ed., *Ireland and the British Empire: Oxford history of the British Empire companion series,* p.139

[142]Capt Mew's son was to later become Director of the Corps of Engineers of the Irish army (1954-1970); Sgt Michael Meehan, *A brief history and compendium of survey company COE* (Irish Defence Forces Printing press, 1999), p.6

[143]Mulcahy papers, MS P7/C/14, also Michael Hopkinson, civil war and aftermath in R. J. Hill, ed., *A new history of Ireland* Vol. VII, Ireland 1921-1984, (Oxford, 2003), p.34

troops to meet the military needs of the Civil War emergency. Men were enlisted without training or medical tests and many were not even issued uniforms. There were many views on the army by prominent figures at the time. It was estimated that of the first 8,000 recruits in the army at the start of the conflict only 6,000 were well armed. The vast majority of these enlisted for the money and not because of a deeper sense of duty. Many, according to General Mulcahy:

'...were from the criminal class' but it was a case of accepting every man who offered his service. The majority of these had to be 'shown how to use a rifle on their way to the areas where fighting was taking place ... and were thrown on their own resources.'[144]

Originally the army raised its strength to 35,000 with 15,000 of these as regular troops and the rest included as volunteer reserves and went about establishing a committee on pay and conditions.[145] A conservative estimate for the size of the Free State Army at the peak of the war and its expansion has been put at 55,000 officers and men. The plans for army expansion and conduct of the ensuing war had been vested by the Free State Government in a three-member war council consisting of General Michael Collins, Commander-in-Chief; General Richard Mulcahy, Minister for Defence and Chief of the General Staff to the Commander-in-Chief, and General Eoin O'Duffy, Assistant Chief of Staff with a larger General Staff of other senior appointments.

Initially the National Army was divided into the five regional commands geographically distributed as the South-Western Command, consisting of Clare, Limerick, Kerry and Cork under the command of General Eoin O'Duffy and assisted by Commandant-General Fionan Lynch and Commandant General W.R.E. Murphy. The

---

[143]Mulcahy papers, MS P7/C/14, also Michael Hopkinson, civil war and aftermath in
   R. J. Hill, ed., *A new history of Ireland* Vol. VII, Ireland 1921-1984, (Oxford, 2003), p.34
[144]Ibid
[145]Raising of army strengths 03 July-04 October 1922, S1302, NAI, Dept of *An Taoiseach* papers Vol. 1

Western Command covered Longford, Roscommon, Westmeath and some areas of Galway, Sligo, Leitrim and Cavan. It came under the control of Major General Sean MacEoin who commanded the midland 2nd, 3rd and 4th Western Divisions. The Eastern Command area was held by the 4th and 5th Northern Divisions, 1st and 2nd Eastern Divisions, Carlow and South Wexford Brigades and was under the control of Major General Emmet Dalton. The South Eastern Command which consisted of Kilkenny, Tipperary-South and Mid-Tipperary as well as Waterford was responsible to Commandant General J.T. Prout and the Curragh Command under Lieutenant-General J.J. O' Connell consisted of the 3rd Southern Division.

All of these senior appointments were made to deal with the developing military situation in Ireland in July, 1922. In time there were many changes but one has to consider that in the beginning each of these divisions and formations, although looking good on paper, needed to be filled with men. These men needed to be found, they needed to be trained, they needed to be equipped, doctrinated and otherwise made into a useful military asset to fight a war to secure a territorial state and also defeat an experienced, armed and successful enemy already in the field. The national army would have to turn to men with experience to train its forces, not least because the anti-Treaty forces were stronger and many dynamic officers of the IRA were now ranged against them including some with foreign experience. There were three types of volunteers in the army: the regular army, the Truce volunteers and the Reserve. The latter being initially recruited for a six-month period as it was hoped this would be enough time for the war to run its course. The people the army wanted were men who would 'flabbergast those who would protract things indefinitely in the country with the intention that the government would never function.'[146]

---

[146]Patrick Long, p.311, UCDA MP P7/B/50

The hierarchy of the new government forces began to appreciate a concept that the post-war British Army had already realised, that a large proportion of recruits who joined after the war were 'ex-soldiers who had acquired a habit of soldiering . . . already trained on enlistment they represented material of the utmost utility.'[147]

On the other hand, a major report on the development of the Irish Army up to 1927, produced by the general staff stated that, 'whereas other armies had the traditions behind them we have not the advantage of experience and even yet are only in the process of building up our traditions.'[148] The report noted that the vast majority of men who entered the army had primary if inadequate knowledge of military duties and discipline because they came from the IRA and had never served in any regular army.[149] Theo Farrell states 'that as a result of experience in the IRA and Ireland's guerrilla warfare, traditions were considered practically useless'.[150] But the Irish Free State Army of 1922-3 did not uniformly fit this description; it fell back on ex-professional and seasoned soldiers and modelled itself on the British Army. The army had been born in the midst of a Civil War and its leaders were too busy building up the forces strength and fighting for survival to consider the shape it would eventually take. They lacked the knowledge to invent their own organisational structure. It was essential that they adopt some foreign system to model themselves upon and since its armament and equipment was British it was the only and ideal model to adopt.[151] The army of January 1922 was essentially the IRA, which had survived the Treaty.

----

[147]Report of the commissioners appointed to inquire into army annual recruiting estimates of effective and non-effective services for the year 1922-3, xii, 46 [C 22 –72], H.C. 1922-3, xiv. 777

[148]Theo Farrell, 'The model army: military imitation and the enfeeblement of the army in post-revolutionary Ireland 1922-42, in *Irish studies in international affairs,* vol. viii, (1997), pp 111-128

[149]Ibid

[150]Ibid

[151]Ibid, p.125

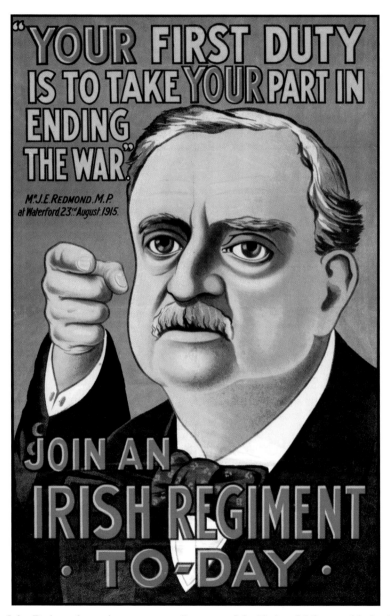

John Redmond recruitment poster. *Courtesy of the National Library of Ireland.*

'Will you answer the call' Great War recruitment poster.
Courtesy of the National Library of Ireland.

Fr. Gleeson Blessing the Munsters. *Courtesy of Schull Books.*

Jack Coveney in British Army uniform.

Jack Coveney's Ypres certificate.

Jack Coveney *(on left)* with some of his army comrades.
The location or date of this picture is not known.

"Emergency' Service certificate of Jack Coveney.
All photographs and certificates pages 72 and 73 courtesy of Dr. Rosaleen Dwyer.

Grave of Coy. Sgt. Major Martin Doyle who was awarded the Victoria Cross. He served in the IRA and national army and is buried under a British military headstone in Grangegorman Cemetery. *Photo Kieran Swords.*

Jim Fitzgerald on left, with ex-British Servicemen on the barge he smuggled IRA weapons upon. *Courtesy of Jimmy Hayles.*

The War of Independence and Great War medals of Jim Fitzgerald. *Courtesy of Jim Hayles.*

Michael Collins grave in Glasnevin Cemetery — surrounded by graves of
Civil War national soldiers. *Photo Kieran Swords.*

The decision to establish a national army in January 1922 was an attempt at confidence building on the part of the Provisional Government even though it knew quite well that it could not rely upon the support of at least half of its members.[152] Collins had even sent senior officers around the country to turn local key IRA men by offering them jobs in the new state's army, police and administration.[153] This would lead to trouble in 1924. Identifying with the Republic he said 'Do you not think I'm as good a republican as Liam Lynch or Liam Deasy. My idea is that if we can get our own army we can tell the British to go to hell'.[154] But there was a divergence of views on Collins and a divergence of loyalties. The general population of the country accepted the Treaty and many local IRA commanders were swayed one way or the other by genuine political conviction.[155]

But Peter Hart points out that after the Treaty and the army's split along the lines of pro-Treaty, Free State National Army forces and anti-Treaty, Republican or IRA forces, the reasons those volunteers went Free State Army are mostly due to their allegiance to Michael Collins. This was the Irish Army in which many ex-British soldiers served.[156] In 1923 an army survey of west Cork concluded that the IRA had survived best where Irregulars had strong family connections.[157] As a result, acute tensions existed inside the army between ex-IRA and ex-British veterans, which was later to develop into the army mutiny of 1924.[158] But acts of comradeship persisted between many army personnel and the IRA and information continually flowed between the lines.[159]

---

[152]Patrick Long, p. 310

[153]Garvin, *Nationalist revolutionaries in Ireland 1858-1928*, p.147

[154]Ibid

[155]Ibid, p.148

[156]Hart, *The IRA and its enemies*, p.265

[157]General situation report 20 September 1923 MAI A/0875

[158]For correspondence relating to hidden forces in Free State army see UCDA, Mulcahy papers P7/C/3,

[159]Tom Garvin, *The birth of Irish democracy*, pp 122-123

Tom Garvin puts forward a theory that the existence of such leakages exaggerated in IRA minds the internal divisions in the army and perhaps lengthened the period of anti-treaty resistance to government forces.[160]

At the beginning the army had no organised presence in most of the country and something was needed to address this and the forces began quickly to expand. Recruitment policy was carefully aimed against reloading the new force with IRA veterans, mostly because of the trust and propaganda issues. According to Mulcahy

> *'policy involved pouring cold water on the idea that the Free State Army was a preserve for any particular self appointed drops of the national cream. On the contrary only select politically trustworthy IRA veterans would be taken and the policy was to absorb into the new force the best of the disbanded British regiments in a way which will get over any stigma on us for them and get them broken up sufficiently to absorb them.'[161]*

Convinced that power corrupts, Republicans and IRA men distrusted politicians; many saw their friends and relatives rushing to share the perks of high office. 'The idea of a professional army cut across their favourite image of a band of brothers, fighting not for personal gain but for an ideal. They saw the spreading stain of materialism as a direct result of English influence.'[162] The absorption of ex-British servicemen occurred easily despite government soldiers occasionally going into battle with shouts of 'up the Leinsters' and 'up the Munsters'.[163] The absorption of Collins's men and the Dublin brigade was a greater problem and they were to be disliked not only by their victims but also

---

[160]Ibid, pp 122-123
[161]Mulcahy papers UCDA P7b/149, P7a/140-2; *Irish Times,* 17 July 1922; Garvin, *The birth of Irish democracy,* p.127
[162]Litton, p.40
[163]Garvin, *The birth of Irish democracy,* p.123

by the bulk of the army. The real problem, however, was that the army had to expand enormously to take control of the territory of the new state.[164] As a consequence much of the army consisted of untrained, raw and unorganised young men for most of the early period.

They were described as being naturally physically brave but ignorant. Officers were unable to read maps, essentially they were ex-IRA guerrilla fighters playing at being regular soldiers, they knew only about street fighting, car bombing and private assassinations.[165] The ex-IRA officers knew no military law. The soldiers were often health hazards because of their filthy habits. Sanitation was very bad and medics were unskilled.[166] There was no disciplinary code until near the end of the war and there was frequent correspondence with GHQ on the standards of government troops.[167] The army was a clumsy tool for restoring order and as such its limitations led to its alienation in some areas around the country with them being described as resembling the Black and Tans.[168] Indeed Harry Boland himself would declare to an acquaintance at the commencement of hostilities on 13 July 1922 that, 'England has again waged war on us . . . this time she has employed Irishmen to do her dirty work . . . the Black and Tans have given way to the Green and Tans. Hamar Greenwood is outdone by Mick Collins.'[169] But if the Republican movement had animosity in its views on the army throughout the conflict it was also having problems of its own with discipline, loyalty and control within the force being major worries at the time.

[164]Ibid, pp 122-123

[165]For criticisms of Irish National army see UCDA, Mulcahy papers P7/B/ 231

[166]Garvin, *The birth of Irish democracy,* pp 122-123

[167]Mulcahy papers, UCDA, P7/B/231

Commandant Peter Young made the compelling points that:

> *'up until this period field commanders had considerable autonomy . . . the centralising of the military forces under a civil authority gradually assumed control . . . not quickly enough in some areas to prevent some atrocities. The problems the army began to have with some of the individuals closest to Collins shows the evolution of a voluntary, fragmented force based on personal loyalties into a professional, regular army loyal to the state'.*[170]

Even with the saturation of ex-British Army war veterans in the army throughout the whole conflict their impact was probably negated in many ways because they were serving in units with untrained and untried soldiers and officers. They were not grouped together into military formations consisting of purely ex-servicemen, led by officers of similar background. If this latter policy had been adopted and they were provided with the proper weaponry, equipment and missions then maybe the course of the conflict might have been different. However Republican propaganda and political intransigence would probably have dealt its punishment again with the prior having a field day. Violence would definitely have been elevated to a higher and unimaginable level and probably extended the duration of the conflict. One question still requires some attention although with an amount of hindsight. Would the political and military atmosphere during the Irish War of Independence in Ireland have been different if the forces of nationalism and republicanism had somehow managed to harness the combined energy, skills and goodwill of the hundreds of thousands of ex-servicemen who came home from the Great War as a resource against Britain?

---

[168]Michael Hopkinson, 'Civil war and aftermath', in *A new history of Ireland* Vol. VII, p.35

[169]Brian P. Murphy, p.299

[170]Comdt Peter Young. 'Michael Collins- A military leader' in *An Cosantoir review 1997: The professional journal of the Defence Forces,* No. 4 (Dublin, 1997), pp 131-142

Many of the previous British administrative structures and practices had merely been taken over by the Irish Free State. Later, with the reformation of the cabinet, W. T. Cosgrave and Kevin O'Higgins, who were seen by Republicans as British puppets, typified the new leaders of the state.

Maryann Valiulis has described the Free State government as:

> '. . . conservative, anti-army, not terribly committed to the ideals of a Gaelic Ireland, they seemed more willing to mould the new state in the image of British society with token gestures thrown to those who clung to the old ideas'.[171]

The Republican hierarchy expected an internal collapse of the Free State. They despised the government because to them it was putatively a British puppet regime.[172] Most importantly, the Republic was disestablished and an oath of allegiance to the British monarch was included in the constitution of the Irish Free State.[173] Sinn Féin and Republicans were themselves essentially conservative; they saw the new army as a modern entity, something of the future and not in keeping with their vision of a Republic. Anti-Treaty literature at this time was full of 1916 metaphors: 'the Republic consecrated by Pearse and Connolly, and the dearest and noblest of our patriots is once more fighting for its life. Citizens defend your Republic.'[174]

[171]Valiulis, p.173

[172]Garvin, *The birth of Irish democracy*, p.125

[173]Garvin, *The birth of Irish democracy*, p.143

[174]MLR Smith, *fighting for Ireland: The Military Strategy of the Irish Republican Movement* (London, 1997), p.50

Comparisons were also made between the new army and RIC:

> *'The RIC were Irishmen to whom England gave arms and orders.*
> *Are you any better? You know in your hearts that Pearse did not die*
> *for the British Empire . . . are you going to murder those who carry*
> *on their work and the holy cause for which they gave their lives.'* [175]

The Provisional Government was accused of being:

> *'a military Junta set up and armed by England in order to wage a*
> *war of aggression against the forces of the Irish Republic . . . The*
> *Free State was in exactly the same position as the British Enemy*
> *were before the truce . . . the machinery is the same, the lying*
> *propaganda, the midnight terrorism, the murder of prisoners of*
> *war, these are England's methods.'* [176]

Tom Garvin described the politics and feelings of the IRA diehard veterans as being 'class derived emotionalism.'[177] Mary McSwiney believed that the pro-Treaty-ites had accepted bribes and Tom Garvin states that in this belief she was 'echoing traditional perceptions of British practice,' a perception which had its roots in the British habit of buying the political support of Irish politicians during the previous two centuries.[178]

These are some of the reasons for the fomenting of republican opinion against ex-servicemen and the army and the prolonging of the Civil War.

---

[175]Ibid
[176]Ibid, p.51
[177]Garvin, *Nationalist revolutionaries in Ireland 1858-1928*, p.126
[178]Ibid, p.161

Chapter IV

'The Free State Army, unlike the armies of other British Commonwealth countries was not made up of lightly renamed versions of the old British regiments. On the contrary those regiments were proudly disbanded. The new Irish Army was actually a strange hybrid organisation consisting of IRA veterans, British Army veterans and young, inexperienced and apolitical mercenaries from the garrison towns who traditionally would have joined the British Army. In many areas it was organised virtually on IRA or Public Band principals during the emergency period of the Civil War but rapidly showed signs of becoming a non-territorial, barrack based regular force of full time professional soldiers.'[179]

Civil War, recruitment and attitudes

Well before the 1927 military mission to the USA, before Fritz Braise and the German and French influences, the Irish Army had already absorbed information from a variety of sources.[180] The IRA itself had standards of training and planning and had earlier modelled itself on the British Army partly in response to British intelligence successes. Later during the Civil War the army carried on the same.[181] Mulcahy and his staff began recruiting for a National Army that would be loyal to the new state.[182] Their uniforms were those of the Volunteers, their insignia was that of the Republic and their members were described as

---

[179]Tom Garvin, 1922: *The Birth of Irish Democracy* (2nd ed., Dublin, 2005), p.122

[180]The Irish army sent a group of officers on a fact finding tour of American military colleges in 1927 with a view to setting up a military school of excellence in Ireland for the professional training of Irish officers; Fritz Braise was an ex-German officer and musician who came to Ireland and being commissioned in the Irish army during the civil war influenced the incorporation of military band music and the military school of music which still exists today

[181]Theo Farrell, p.126

[182]Valiulis, p. 128

pre-Truce veterans but despite these similarities, it was a new army. From its inception the army followed regular military procedure, wore uniforms, lived in barracks, learned drill and standard tactics and was armed with British weapons.[183] Republican's claimed they were fighting the same enemy they just had different uniforms.[184] Neither side had money to fight a war, but the government was supported by Britain.[185]

Despite this, many army commanders felt unable to control their units and the camaraderie and fraternity between their men and those of the anti-Treaty side jeopardised the army's effectiveness.[186] The loose structure of the old Volunteer force made it difficult for many to adapt to the demands of a regular army.

The employment of ex-British officers became a necessity.[187] One of these was Colonel Dan Coghlan, a former British officer who had been decorated by the British and French governments for work in the graves registration and who had war experience. Michael Collins prevailed on him upon the outbreak of the Civil War to return to Ireland and join the new army. Coughlan stayed close to Collins throughout the conflict and was a pallbearer at his funeral.[188]

This officer was no doubt an advisor to Collins at certain times and was obviously highly respected enough to be head hunted by the Irish military establishment in the hope that he and others would have a positive impact. This was one reason for the recruitment of ex-servicemen to bolster the army.[189]

---

[183]Ibid.

[184]Carlton Younger, *Ireland's Civil War* (2nd ed., London, 1886), p.235

[185]Younger, p.278

[186]Ibid, p.130

[187]Michael Hopkinson, *Green Against Green* (2nd ed. Dublin, 2004), p.138

[188]O' Farrell, p.149

[189]Dalton was tasked with recruiting from Legion of Ex-Servicemen; Meda Ryan, *The Day Michael Collins was Shot* (Dublin, 1989), p.25

This worked to a great extent because the army later showed little loyalty to former IRA members who sided with them against the Republicans, but who were later demobilised because they were not deemed professional.[190]

The employment of ex-British soldiers in reality was purely a utility. During the war army efficiency and discipline did improve rapidly in certain areas. New officers with British and other foreign experience were sharpening things up in the provinces.[191] General W.R.E. Murphy, Director of Operations was doing 'remarkable work in Kerry, which went from being one of the most disaffected areas in the state to one of the quietest.'[192]

The signing of the Treaty on 6 December 1921, had been the signal for the disbandment of the five Southern Irish regiments of the British Army. It was asked 'how can there remain in the British Army regiments essentially Irish in every way under present conditions therefore they must go at once'.[193] This was timely for the new Irish Army. In January 1922, Lieutenant General E. P. Strickland signed special orders for the breaking up the sixth division of the British Army in Southern Ireland.[194] The British War Office declared the Irish command abolished, effective from December 17 1922.[195]

Major General Burton Foster; Colonel of the Royal Irish said:

> ' . . . where a Free State exists the troops must belong to the Free State'.[196]

---

[190]Theo Farrell, p.126

[191]Garvin, *The Birth of Irish Democracy,* p.125

[192]Garvin, *The Birth of Irish Democracy,* p.125

[193]*The Irish Times,* 14 Jan. 1922

[194]Florence O'Donohue papers, NLI, MS. 31, 232,

[195]*The Irish Times,* 6 Jan. 1923

[196]Patrick McCarthy, p.333

The Irish Regiments of the British Army who were traditionally recruited in Southern Ireland and which were disbanded in 1922 were the Royal Irish Regiment (18th of Foot), the Connaught Rangers (88th & 94th of Foot), the Prince of Wales Leinster Regiment (Royal Canadians) (100th of Foot), the Royal Munster Fusiliers (101st & 104th of Foot), the Royal Dublin Fusiliers (102nd & 103rd of Foot)) and the South Irish Horse (Special Reserve). All were famous Irish military formations of the British Army.[197] The other Irish Regiments of the British Army went through a series of amalgamations, which carried on to the late 1960s. By February 1922, the new Irish Army was recruiting ex-British soldiers with specialist skills.[198]

In July 1922 the Freeman's Journal had published a poster titled:

FLOCK TO THE FLAG
HEAVY RESPONSE TO IRISH GOVERNMENT
CALL TO ARMS
IRISH ARMY AUTHORITIES PLANS

The appeal of the Irish government for volunteers has met with a most gratifying response.

TRAINED MEN

Preference is being given to old members of the Irish Volunteers of good character. Next to them will be considered the applications of men who are able to handle firearms. Many of the applicants yesterday bore the stamp of ex-servicemen, who have seen strenuous war duty in other lands.[199]

---

[197]Brigadier A. E. C. Bredin DSO, MC, DL, *A history of the Irish soldier,* (Belfast, 1987), p.549

[198]For an example of a recruitment poster see O' Malley papers P17a/257, UCDA; *Freeman's Journal,* 6 July 1922; recruitment for 12 month period *The Irish Times,* 23 Jan. 1923

[199]*Freeman's Journal,* 8 July 1922

On 5 July 1922, the Provisional Government opened recruitment for five Dublin battalions and local commanders throughout the country were authorised to accept recruits. On the first day in Dublin, officers were unable to deal with the large number of applicants. Eoin Neeson points out that this was due to the large volume of unemployed ex-soldiers anxious to continue a life to which they were accustomed.[200]

Recruitment was at 1,000 a day and a large proportion of the criminal element found its way in, as well as old soldiers experienced in every kind of military wrongdoing, who were placed under the command of inexperienced officers.[201] Even where good, experienced soldiers were concerned, some became undisciplined by being placed under inexperienced leaders.

Officers of the Volunteers who had remained loyal to the state were re-commissioned in the army. Others with no connections to the Volunteers, i.e. ex-British servicemen, were commissioned to train recruits and officers. Men were also commissioned for posting to the technical corps (railway protection, repair, coastal & marine engineers etc).[202] These soldiers were important in the Civil War.[203]

These ex-British servicemen were more than entitled to join and serve in the new National Army. After all they were military trained Irishmen, with the emphasis being placed on Irishmen. They were essential as instructors and combatants as they had experience and some had also been in the IRA. As Niall Harrington pointed out Emmet Dalton, W.R.E. Murphy, Dermot McManus and A.T. Lawlor

---

[200]Eoin Neeson, *Birth of a Republic,* (Dublin, 1998), p.293

[201]Ibid, p.293

[202]Ministry of defence memorandum for the army inquiry committee dated 17 Apr. 1924, Mulcahy papers P7/B/5 + 54, for memorandum on reorganisation and structure of army see P7/B/189, P7/B/190, UCDA

[203]Scheme for organisation and training of engineers in Mulcahy papers UCDA P7/B/52

(later General Officer Commanding the Curragh) all had distinguished service in the British Army prior to joining the pre-Truce IRA and now held senior positions.[204]

According to Peter Hart most army recruits were either ex-British soldiers or civilians and many of them were unemployed labourers.[205] One example of their recruitment comes from a memorandum on the army inquiry dated 17 April 1924. It refers to the Railway Protection & Repair & Maintenance Corps and states 'as the corps grew a certain number of ex-officers of Irish regiments of the British Army were given commissions'.[206]

The recruitment for the army could be sporadic. A report to the cabinet in October 1922, details how General W.R.E. Murphy while operating in Kerry, was to recruit ex-servicemen, not more than 200 and not after 1 November, 1922.[207] In the same report the army's strength was put at 25,000 with 2,286 in various stages of training in special services such as signals, engineers and with Lewis gunners being especially sought.[208]

There may also have been transfers of men between the British and Irish forces as this letter from General Sean McEoin suggests:

> *'Soldier named Fred Cantlone RASC military transport company, fifteen years service, whole time in transport, thirty nine years old, five and a half years to go to pension and is now under orders to proceed to Belfast. He is anxious to transfer to Irish Army. Saw active service in France & Italy, has much experience'.*[209]

---

[204]Niall Harrington, *Kerry landing August 1922: An episode of the civil war* (Dublin, 1992), p.37

[205]Hart, *The IRA and its enemies,* p.264

[206]Ibid

[207]Report to cabinet dated 16 Oct. 1922, UCDA Mulcahy papers P7/B/258-259

[208]Ibid

[209]Sean McEoin Papers, UCDA, P151/149,

But the army rushed people into action without any real preparation for combat operations. 'Men were taught the mechanisms of a rifle very often on the way to a fight.'[210]

As regards the training and suitability for combat of government soldiers one can get an idea of the preparation of men with no experience and the need for experienced people from a reply to a question asked of Kevin O' Higgins, Minister of Home Affairs at the time:

> '. . . on the general conditions as regards recruiting for the National Army there was no definite period of training for recruits outside of large cities such as Dublin, Cork and Limerick until recently. A large number of men did however go through a purely training period of four to eight weeks at the Curragh. Once outside the Curragh, the responsible officer in charge of his unit was satisfied that a man was fit to handle a gun properly, he was liable for ordinary duty.'[211]

Between 28 June and 6 July 1922, sixty-two National soldiers were killed and 277 had been injured.[212] In October it was reported that twenty-four officers and men had died of wounds received accidentally from 1 June 1922 and steps were taken to instruct troops in the proper use of arms.[213]

But the ordinary recruit or government soldier had very inadequate weapons training and the hierarchy did not understand the quality and capabilities of their men, or which type of men they had at their disposal for that matter. For instance the 'ad hoc' training regime of the army can be further revealed through the activities of No. 1 Company of the Special Infantry Corps (SIC) based in Renmore Barracks in Galway in early 1923.

---

[210]Litton, p. 90

[211]*Dail Eireann debates,* parliamentary debates; official report, vol. I, 6 Dec. - 27 Mar. 1923 (Dublin Stationary Office, 1922), p.2023

[212]*Freeman's Journal,* 7 July. 1922

[213]*The Irish Times,* 21 Oct. MP UCDA 1922; P7/B/218

The SIC had been formed earlier that year to combat the serious increase in crime and was based throughout the country. The Renmore company commander Capt. Higgins, on being instructed to carry out intensive training periods for his men complained that he did not have sufficient time to do this because of his workload on patrolling his area of responsibility. He had, however, managed to facilitate some basic close and extended order squad drill on the barrack square as well as some rifle exercises and bayonet fighting instruction. But when he asked for permission to fire live ammunition on the range the corps second in command replied that 'When you are satisfied that it will not be a waste of ammunition, you can certainly give them five rounds each.' Ironically this officer need not have worried as it was later realised that practically all of the men in the unit had British Army service.[214] Had this unit been provided with the proper leadership and equipment it might have made a unique impact.

The senior staff of the army and General Emmett Dalton, an ex-British officer, had been corresponding with a Mr. Walker of the Legion of Irish ex-Servicemen to supply ex-British soldiers for service in the army to train its men.[215] An order for five hundred artillerymen, machine gunners, engineers and signallers was made by GHQ and a further list for instructors, weapons experts, military policemen, armourers, aircraft riggers and fitters, drivers and medical personnel to be recruited. The instructors would receive £5 per week with no specific military rank. They would receive an officer's uniform without rank insignia and maintained at army expense. Other services would be remunerated at rates of pay equal to regular army rates. Technicians would receive extra allowances. Those who previously held rank would retain those ranks. Most of the instructors Walker produced were senior NCOs with up to twenty-nine years service and

---

[214]Anthony Kinsella, 'Organisation and development of the pro-Treaty forces 1922-1924,' in special edition of the *Irish Sword: The journal of the military history society of Ireland. Titled the Civil War 1922-23,* Vol. XX. No. 82 (Dublin, 1997), pp 331-348
[215]Patrick McCarthy, p.334

a variety of skills.[216] The NCO Corps was the backbone of the British Army. Its successes in conflict during the nineteenth and early twentieth centuries was due to their quality and ability to perform and continually rise to the demands set upon them.'[217] The supply of ex-servicemen continued in spite of regular anti- British sentiments in certain areas. However some men were inevitably rejected because their old allegiances were too proudly worn and would have caused disharmony within the army.

By the end of July 1922 there were 2,484 reservists in training.[218] This recruitment led to an influx of people to the army with some deserting the British forces to join up. In 1923 the British and Irish governments agreed to exchange information on ex-members of the British forces serving in the army.[219] Many had deserted for enlistment in Ireland, which carried on throughout the Civil War and after the mutiny.[220] The British estimated in 1923 that 5,000 of their soldiers had disappeared in Ireland since 1916 but this was disputed.[221] Some of them would have been casualties of the ongoing conflict, i.e. those killed or murdered and buried, those who deserted and decided to live peacefully and those who joined the IRA and National Army during the intervening years. One report alone listed thirty-four deserters who were serving in the army in one area.[222] Some soldiers were inevitably victims of the violence, which was such a dramatic element of the period but evidence shows that many joined the government forces of the Free State.

[216]Mulcahy papers, UCDA, P7/B/9

[217]Victor Neuburg, 'Backbone of the British army: NCOs Until 1900' in *The army quarterly and defence Journal,* Vol.124, No 24 (Devon, 1994), pp 412-416

[218]Patrick Long, p. 312

[219]NAI Memorandum no 138 S.2140

[220]Dept of Taoiseach files NAI, desertion from British army in Ireland general file, 29 Feb. 1924 - 7 Feb. 1925, S.3694

[221]Dept of Taoiseach papers S.3644 NAI, letter from Attorney General Tim Healy to no 10 Downing St governor general's file

[222]Dept of Taoiseach files F.71, NAI, Colonial Office dispatch 11 June 1924 governor general's file S.3644

The new Irish Army reported to the Colonial Office that many British reservists were applying to join the Free State Army and sought guidance. The British replied in the positive but with the caveat which reiterated that they would have first claim on these men in time of national mobilisation, especially those on the naval reserve and this was already agreed to by General Mulcahy and the Irish government on 22 November 1922.[223] Some men receiving medical pensions due to injuries received during the Great War had joined the Free State Army and the British government wanted certain categories of them discharged and their names transmitted to the British Ministry of Pensions. Furthermore the ministry of pensions outlined that it would no longer undertake to provide treatment for any Great War pensioner during his time in service of the National Army for injuries suffered therein.[224] Processes and procedures were put in place to discharge reservists from their commitments when they joined the Irish Free State Army with some joining the Coastal Defence Forces. The government agreed to arrest and hand over deserters to the British military authorities.[225]

In response to the question regarding those in receipt of medical pensions who were serving in the national forces the British authorities were informed that,

> '. . . during the recent national emergency men were accepted for active service who would not normally be regarded as medically suitable for enlistment and no information was sought as to receipt or otherwise by them of disability pensions in respect of service in the Imperial forces'[226]

---

[223]Governor Generals files NAI, F.71, Colonial Office dispatch 28 February 1923 from Secretary of State for the Colonies to Governor General Irish Free State

[224]Ibid

[225]Dept of *An Taoiseach* files NAI, F.71, Governor General dispatch 526 to Colonial Office; British Military & Naval reservists in Saorstat Eireann 28 Nov 1922-18 Feb 1927 S.3238 + S. 1896 + S.5438

[226]Dept of *An Taoiseach* files NAI, F.71, Dispatch to Colonial Office number 138 dated 31 August 1923, S. 2140

This further illustrates the 'ad hoc' approach to recruitment and commitment of untried and untrained men into combat by the National Army. Other ex-servicemen joined the army who did not necessarily fit the bill as regards being fighting fit. They did however have an impact as they found employment in offices, stores and other logistical areas, which were equally important in keeping a semblance of a proficient military system afloat.

For instance Private Henry Stewart had been recruited into the army on 5 January 1923, in Clarke Barracks, Curragh camp, Co. Kildare. His discharge papers from Óglaigh na hÉireann on 26 March 1929, show that he had served six years and eighty-one days and was discharged in consequence of being medically unfit for army service.[227] According to his papers he had served in the 8th Infantry Battalion as a clerk during those years and his character was described as being very good.

What is very interesting about Henry Stewart is that he had joined the army midway through the Civil War and he had survived the conflict and the demobilisation that saw thousands let go that might have wished to stay on. He was a lowly private soldier in the scheme of things but who was obviously good and responsible at his job and managed to stay in the army through the various reorganisations of the 1924 period right up until 1929. What is unusual is that his discharge papers state that he was fifty years old when he was attested, in fact he was fifty-six, which means he was sixty-two years of age when he retired.

Recruitment of older men for service in the army was nothing new as the British military had conscripted thousands of middle-aged and older men in the latter part of the Great War when the supply began to dry up due to the attrition of the war. When the Irish Army recruited Henry and possibly many others like him it was recognising their experience and skills.

---

[227] I am extremely grateful to Margaret Stewart, granddaughter of Henry Stewart, who provided this information and allowed me to use extracts from her unpublished compilation of his diary and papers.

From his granddaughter's compilation of his diary and papers it is possible to offer a brief history of Henry's military career. At age eighteen he originally enlisted in the Royal Dublin Fusiliers in Naas, Co. Kildare on 12 December 1884 serving seven years with another five on reserve. He was stationed at Naas throughout 1884 to 1886, in Mullingar in 1887, the Curragh between 1888 and 1890 and in Newry in 1891. In 1894 he was recalled to Naas for training as a reservist and was sent to South Africa where he saw action in 1900 and 1901 as part of the military forces during the Second Anglo Boer War 1899-1902. During World War One he was stationed in Edinburgh with the Labour Corps and is thought to have served in France and was later admitted to the Curragh Military Hospital during 1916 and 1917.

A letter from Lieutenant Colonel Robinson, a liaison officer of the Royal Dublin Fusiliers, to the Local Government Board for Ireland and dated 16 April 1919 states that:

> '. . . *Pte. Henry Stewart served in the battalion under my command for over three years during which time he was for a considerable time in charge of regimental stores, and always proved himself a most conscientious, trustworthy, sober, honest and hardworking old soldier and I shall feel extremely pleased to hear of his obtaining suitable employment. . .'*[228]

The Irish army employed Henry in 1923, where his skills were put to good use and if it were not for the important research carried out by his granddaughter and his family history being recorded, it would have been lost.

Another example of the continuation of service of a soldier in both the British and Irish armies is the career of John Augustin Coveney. Jack, as he was known, was born on 23rd June 1894 in Cork and enlisted as a rifleman with the 3rd Battalion Kings Royal Rifle Corps in Lancaster, England. He saw active service in the Great War, including

---

[228]Margaret Stewart, unpublished compilation of Henry Stewart's diary

the fighting at Ypres and carried scars on his right forearm, back and both legs. After the war he was transferred to the army reserve in February, 1919.

Like thousands of others, Jack returned to Cork but could not settle back into his old life and in August of the same year he returned to the colours and was posted to the British garrison at Mhow, Indore in Northern India. Soon afterwards he met his future wife Katherine (Kitty) Crosbie. When she returned to Dublin Jack left the army and followed her home to be married. He had been discharged from the British Army on 24 November 1922 and enlisted with the new Irish Army in Dublin on 19 March 1923. He was twenty eight years old and had joined at the height of the Irish Civil War serving in Athlone, Ballina, Tralee and Limerick among other places.

In April 1930 Jack left full time service and was posted to the reserve list where he remained until April 1939. Not long afterwards Jack was once again in uniform when he served in Collins Barracks, Cork during the Irish Emergency period of the Second World War. With his time in both the British and Irish military Jack had served almost twenty six years on both full time and reserve service as an infantryman, a motor mechanic and cook and he attained the rank of sergeant.[229]

Many other veterans transcended the old social forms and taboos and joined the IRA and Irish Army after surviving the carnage of the greatest war in history. William Henry in his study of soldiers of the Great War wrote about Sergeant Edward John Carr of the Royal Inniskillen Fusiliers. Born in Donegal on 14 October 1894, he lived all his life in Galway enlisting when war broke out in 1914. He was wounded in both legs and taken prisoner and as he was a tailor by trade, he was put to this work in the camp. After returning home

---

[229]Courtesy of Dr. Rosaleen Dwyer

Edward joined the IRA during the Irish War of Independence and later enlisted in the National Army where he remained until retirement.[230] Private Joe Leonard of the Black Watch was born in 1894 in Prospect Hill, Galway and educated at St Ignatius College. He too was severely wounded at the Battle of the Somme on 1 July, 1916, not long after the insurrection in Dublin. By 1917, he had joined Sinn Féin and shortly afterwards became a senior member of the IRA. According to his family Joe ranked amongst the ten most wanted men in Ireland during the War of Independence.[231]

Joe Madden of the Royal Engineers was born in 1871 at Garybreeda, Loughrea and enlisted in February 1915. He left his large young family to take part in the great Somme offensive of 1916. After the war he became 'embroiled in the national conflict with his home being raided on more than one occasion by the Black and Tans'.[232] Connaught Ranger Private Pat Purcell from Isserkelly, Ardrahan became involved in the national struggle and later joined the government forces during the Irish Civil War.[233] So also did Lance Corporal Michael White from Portumna who was a military chiropodist and who had served in the Boer War and India. He was awarded the South Africa campaign medal and bars and the Good Conduct Medal later serving in the Irish Army as a chiropodist for a number of years. His brother was killed in the Great War.[234]

There were even navy men like Able Seaman John O'Brien from the Claddagh in Galway. He was a signalman in the Royal Navy and this was a skill that was sought after by the new National Army in Ireland, which he later joined.[235] All of these men had reasons to go to war in

---

[230]William Henry, *Forgotten heroes: Galway soldiers of the Great War 1914-1918* (Cork, 2007), pp 36-37
[231]Ibid, p.55
[232]Ibid, p.57
[233]Ibid, p.64
[234]Ibid, p.67
[235]Ibid, p.61

Europe and then to join the struggle for Irish freedom, some were involved in almost ten years of constant conflict. It is one of the aspects of the period which has never been fully examined.

Impact of ex-British soldiers on Irish National Army

Most veterans did not leave records of their experiences. As such there is a remarkable absence of any great analytical work on the ex-British soldier serving in the Irish Army during the period. Probably one of the more noteworthy exceptions of these is Major General W.R.E. Murphy.[236] William Richard English Murphy (1890-1975) was born in Wexford. On the outbreak of the First World War he joined the British Army.[237] He saw action including the Battles of Loos and the Somme where on the first day of July, 1916 he was tasked with leading a bombing team to clear fortified enemy positions in the village of Mamets. Of the Battalion's 21 officers who went over the top that morning six were killed and five were wounded by the end of the day. In 1918 Murphy was promoted to Lieutenant Colonel and was then an Irish Catholic officer commanding a battalion of English soldiers, namely the 1st battalion South Staffordshire regiment.

On 27 October that same year, as part of the British 10th Army, his unit was involved in the final offensive of the war in Italy. He was awarded the Distinguished Service Order for his actions during the Battle of Vittoro Veneto.This involved a direct assault across the Piave, a fast-flowing river in Venetia, the opposite side of which was held by well-entrenched troops of the Austro-Hungarian Army. His unit was one of those tasked with assaulting the enemy positions on the far bank and this looked like it would be a costly venture. Murphy changed the plans of the attack which he was given, just enough to give his men a better chance at success and survival with minimum casualties.

---

[236]Karl Murphy, 'An Irish general: William Richard English Murphy, 1890-1975', in *History Ireland,* vol. xiii no.3 (Dublin, 2005), pp 10-11
[237]Ibid

They went on to capture their objectives as well as a number of villages and over 2,800 enemy soldiers and equipment.[238] This would certainly not have been the result if he had pursued the original plan.

On the outbreak of the Irish Civil War and at the request of Collins and others he took up a position in the Irish Army.[239] Initially Murphy conducted a course for senior officers at the Curragh during the summer of 1922.[240] Some of these officers resented taking instruction from an ex-British soldier and departed with some ending up on the Republican side during the Civil War.[241] He commanded troops under the direction of Eoin O'Duffy, organising attacks on Republican forces in Bruree and Kilmallock in Co. Limerick during September 1922 after the fighting in Dublin.[242] The forces of General Prout and Colonel Paul had been steadily pushing the Eastern end of the Republican 'Waterford-Limerick Line' as General's O'Duffy and Murphy were pushing its Western end.[243] A report to GHQ congratulated Murphy's handling of the action saying 'he must be given the credit for a well conceived and well executed attack.'[244] In a statement to the press it was pointed out that he 'considered the capture of Bruree of much strategic value making Kilmallock untenable.'[245] In Tralee in November 1922 he spared the lives of four IRA activists who had been sentenced to death for possession of weapons.[246] Murphy had the sentences changed to penal servitude.[247]

---

[238]Ibid

[239]Ibid.

[240]Karl Murphy, 'General W.R.E. Murphy and the Irish Civil War' (M.A. thesis, NUI Maynooth, 1996), p.3

[241]Ibid, p. 3

[242]Murphy was contacted by General Gearoid O' Sullivan in 1922 and asked for advice in setting up a national army, Karl Murphy, (M.A. thesis)

[243]George Morison, *The Irish Civil War: An illustrated history,* (Dublin, 1981), p.75

[244]Ibid

[245]Mulcahy papers, UCDA, P7/B/68; Murphy, unpublished thesis

[246]Mulcahy papers, UCDA, P7/B/101

[247]Mulcahy papers, UCDA, 7/B/72

The day after he departed from his Kerry command *An Phoblacht* carried an article on him saying:

'*He was the man who had the power of life and death under English imperial authority, he never took any part in the Irish movement . . . he was never a Volunteer man, never a Gaelic Leaguer and never in the Sinn Fein movement . . . the man who was in charge of what is humorously called "the army of the people" in the Kerry area.*' [248]

However, Murphy's personal conduct in Kerry was unblemished by accusations of mistreatment unlike other IRA accusations towards Free State officers such as O'Daly.[249]

Lieutenant Colonel Tommy Ryan, assistant to Murphy as deputy GOC operations and training was sent to the Curragh for further training by General O'Daly of the Dublin brigade in early January 1923, soon after Murphy's departure. O'Daly, a Collins man, knew Ryan had commanded a British battalion in France and the Middle East during the Great War and had been a brigade commander in Egypt in 1918 and this was seen as a total insult to him.[250] Ryan was well trained and had plenty of experience of warfare where O'Daly's experience of a conventional army was nil. Connor Brady notes that 'Murphy was both as brilliant and skilful a soldier as he was an administrator' as Ryan would have been.[251] But not everyone agreed, especially some contemporary IRA leaders. Ernie O'Malley recounts an incident where

---

[248]*An Phoblacht,* 3 Jan. 1923

[249]References to the Ballyseedy atrocity in which eight republicans were murdered by Free State troops, Karl Murphy, (M.A. thesis), p.49; Joe Galvin an ex-Irish Guards soldier was killed in this incident

[250]Mulcahy papers, UCDA, P7/C/4; Karl Murphy's theory, Karl Murphy, (M.A. thesis), p.56

[251]Connor Brady, *Guardian's of the peace* (Dublin, 1974)

he knew the movements and actions of Murphy in advance because he had a good grasp of the man's thinking. He said 'he could also see that Murphy could move his formations across a map quicker than on rough terrain.'[252]

Frank Aiken said:

> 'The Free State preen themselves on the result of O'Duffy's campaign. From a military point of view the strategy of the whole Free State campaign was good but the commanders in the field did not handle men in action as well as ours . . . they relied on sheer weight of lead rather than O'Duffy's or W.R.E. Murphy's tactics.'[253]

Trying to get an untrained military force to take orders and carry out missions properly was no easy task. Murphy's problem was changing a guerrilla force into an efficient regular army. His preparations for the attack on Kilmallock were hampered by a lack of basic military training in the army. Consternation erupted at one stage when Murphy ordered trenches to be dug.[254] Soldiers did not know how to go about this basic military function and probably couldn't be bothered with a laborious and intensive task such as that. General O'Duffy had also complained to GHQ that 'the 300 reserve soldiers sent to his command in July proved absolutely worthless. At least 200 of them never handled a rifle before, were never in the Volunteers or the British Army.'[255] In Tralee, a Captain Roche had to repeatedly arrest drunken officers who would subsequently be released from their confines by untrained or friendly soldiers. Discipline was very poor and inconsistent. The British Expeditionary Force (BEF) had learnt at the

---

[252] Ernie O' Malley, *The singing flame*, p.168
[253] Frank Aiken to MacSwiney 29 Apr. 1924, UCDA, p104/1317; Fearghal McGarry, *Eoin O'Duffy: A self made hero* (Oxford, 2005), p.110
[254] Mulcahy papers, UCDA, P7/B/68
[255] General O' Duffy to GHQ, 4 Aug 1922 Mulcahy papers, UCDA, P7/B/08

beginning of the Great War that training and discipline were essential and 'how concealment of a khaki uniform and the ability to read a map under enemy fire were essential parts of an officer's experience as the British Army retreated before a powerful enemy.'[256] The Irish Army was slowly learning this lesson too.

Some units, including the Dublin Guards and the 1st Western Division, were good, but the army needed more people with experience. It was advised that 50 per cent of the officers should be demobbed along with 20 per cent of the troops and that units of ex-British Army members be formed. It was stated that ex-British NCOs were the best for getting work out of troops.[257] But later on, General O'Duffy spoke on the topic of a saturation of ex-soldiers. He was worried about the lack of patriotism and *'espirit de corps'* within the army. 'The only tales that young recruits were likely to hear about past deeds of Irish soldiers in this mercenary army', as he called it, 'were accounts of the Dublin's in Gallipoli from the lips of some ex-British NCO'[258]

He argued that:

> *'the army should exploit its rich military tradition and suggested that each battalion select a notable patriot whose portrait would be hung in the mess and whose history the soldiers would study. The result would provide 'something more than a third rate imitation of the British Army dressed in green uniforms and a higher ideal to fight for than a pay envelope.'*[259]

---

[256]Soldiers and Chief's military exhibition in National Museum of Ireland

[257]Mulcahy papers, UCDA, P7a/141

[258]McGarry, p.138

[259]General O'Duffy to executive council 30 Sept 1924, UCDA, P24/222

A contemporary report says:

> '*having observed General Murphy as a leader in the field, as an organiser and as a strategist, I believe him to be the most capable officer I have ever met. He is, in addition, popular among the troops, an intelligent disciplinarian and in short, in my belief the one man capable of finishing the campaign. The loss of General Murphy would be more disastrous than the loss of 4,000 troops.*'[260]

During the war other ex-servicemen came to prominence. In July 1923, Major General John T. Prout attacked republican forces in Waterford city.[261] These positions covered the River Suir, which spanned 250 yards, using the waterfront as their line of defence.[262]

Colonel Patrick Paul, another ex-soldier, produced a plan to cross up river to attack the republican left flank and used artillery to harass their positions. He wanted to 'break the enemy's morale as they had no experience of shellfire, and the effects of high explosives on men who had never known them can be imagined.'[263] However, this did not stop him inadvertently destroying his own house in the city with his own artillery barrage.[264]

All during the period ex-British soldiers serving in the army were fighting and sustaining casualties both fatalities and injuries, just like others in the force. In August, 1922, Captain T. J. McNabola was wounded at Boyle. He had served during the European War with the South Irish Horse and the Machinegun Corps.[265]

---

[260]Ibid, Karl Murphy believes that the author of the report may have been Kingsmill Moore, the *Irish Times* war correspondent, who had been covertly sending back reports to Desmond Fitzgerald and Kevin O' Higgins, Murphy M.A. thesis

[261]Paul V. Walsh, *The Irish Civil War 1922-1924*

[262]Ibid; Carlton Younger, p. 138

[263]Ibid; Duggan, p. 89

[264]*Freeman's Journal*, 20 July. 1922

[265]*Freeman's Journal*, 8 July. 1922

In August, Tom O'Keefe was killed in a roadside ambush near Mullinavat.[266] Ernie O'Malley describes many of the wounded soldiers he encountered, while he himself was as an injured prisoner in a military hospital, as being 'sympathetic and offered to help in any way they could . . . many of them were soldiers of the world war.'[267] It was also here that O'Malley was introduced, through one of its veterans, to the complexities of the Connaught Rangers mutiny, which had taken place in India. The ex-Ranger lay injured, a government soldier and therefore, a supposed enemy, in the bed next to him, O'Malley although very anti-English, seemed to make time for the soldiers. But when they castigated Erskine Childers on hearing of his capture and repeated the widespread rhetoric of his being 'that damned reactionary spy of an Englishman' O'Malley became upset and tried to explain the importance and influence of the man to them. 'They knew nothing about him except what their officers told them.'[268] O'Malley's Connaught Ranger, who was rather more experienced and sympathetic, brought in a revolver and placed it under the Republican leaders mattress for him to use if he should attempt to escape 'that's for you when you're able to use it' he said, but O'Malley never got the chance as he was too weak and was moved soon after to another location.[269]

Another extraordinary career is that portrayed in the case of Company Sergeant Major Martin Doyle a former British soldier.[270] He was one of the twenty-nine Irish Victoria Cross winners of the First World War.

---

[266]*Irish Times,* 17 Aug. 1922
[267]Ernie O'Malley, *The singing flame,* p.192
[268]Ibid, p.193
[269]Ibid, p.195
[270]*Wexford People,* 13 Dec. 1990; Byrne, Cpl, Liam, 'An Irish soldier remembered, in *An Cosantóir: The Defence Forces magazine, special 1916 edition* (Dublin, 1991), pp 28-31
[269]Ibid
[270]Duggan, pp 110-111

He retired from the British Army in 1919 and immediately joined the IRA. He served as an intelligence officer in the mid Clare brigade throughout 1920-1921 spending long periods on the run. After the Truce he joined the army and was described as someone who could not be replaced without serious inconvenience to the service.[271]

Chaplains

In June 1922, it became appropriate to attach chaplains to army formations at the request of local commanders. By November of that year a defence order readjusted the figure to twenty seven full time chaplains in the service of the National Army. By January 1923 a Command Chaplain supervised the work in each command and it is interesting to note that promiscuity was seen as a bigger problem than drink among the men.[272] A number of these chaplains had Great War experience including one man in particular Fr. Francis Gleeson. He served with the 2nd Battalion of the Munster Fusiliers.

During his time as chaplain to this unit Fr. Gleeson became very popular with the men through his deep compassion as well as his skill with the mouth organ. He was well known for supplying vast quantities of these instruments to soldiers in the trenches and for delivering fiery uplifting talks in which nationality and religion played a huge part.[273]

But Gleeson is probably best remembered for being portrayed as the centrepiece of Fortunino Matania's famous painting titled "The last Absolution of the Munsters at Rue de Bois, 1915". The painting depicts the blessing of the Royal Munster Fusiliers on the evening of 8 May by their chaplain Fr Gleeson, mounted on horseback in front of a ruined shrine holding a crucifix aloft to bless the troops. Each company has a green standard embroidered with an Irish harp and the word "Munster".

---

[271]Ibid
[272]Duggan, pp 110-111
[273]Myles Dungan pp66,73

The 2nd Battalion attacked from their trenches at dawn the following day. In the battle that ensued the battalion dead numbered 381 including the commanding officer and his adjutant. Gleeson never forgot the experiences of the war and on his return to Ireland he joined the Irish Army chaplaincy service, no doubt coming across many former comrades. Later he took up residency in one of Dublin's inner city parishes where he managed to construct a shrine in memory of the war. At the outbreak of World War Two, Fr Gleeson was said to have taken the prospect of Ireland becoming embroiled very seriously and as a result began a vigil of prayer and retreat so that this would not occur.[274]

The Free State Air Force

The Irish Air Corps as we know it today had its origins in 1922 when a general Routine Order was published inviting young officers to apply to transfer from the army to the Department of Aviation whose HQ was in Beggars Bush Barracks, Dublin. The two initial officers of the newly formed Irish Free State Army Air Corps were Major Generals Charles Russell and Jack McSweeney. Both had seen service with the Royal Flying Corps in the Great War and had IRA War of Independence service and were found suitable for a secret mission through enquiries within the Dublin brigade.[275] Russell had served with No. 65 Squadron in France and McSweeney with No. 50 Squadron RFC. The first aircraft was a five-seater biplane, a Martinsyde type A Mk II.[276] Based in England it had been purchased from the Aircraft Disposal Company at Croydon by the Irish Self Determination League in collaboration with the Provisional Government in December 1921, in the guise of the Canadian Forestry Department.

---

[274]Fr Gleeson served in St Catherine's Church in Dublin city and he is buried in
   Glasnevin cemetery
[275]*Irish Independent*, 11 Mar. 1965
[276]*Irish Independent*, 4 July. 1997

The plan involved McSweeney flying the aircraft and Russell and a group of Volunteers securing a landing area. Then if the treaty talks should fail they would bring Michael Collins back to Ireland.[277] The aircraft had been kept on standby in England and the men were ready for an escape mission that would make history. The pilots had to increasingly come up with spurious problems with the aircraft so that McSweeney would not have to sign for it and in this way prolong the acceptance long enough for the talks in London to finalise, or at least for the plan to be ready. In the end the planned for historic escape did not transpire.

By April 1922 the aerodrome at Baldonnel was occupied by government troops and recruitment began. Ned Broy, who later became Garda Commissioner, was a member of the old administration and was very instrumental in the planning and purchase of the Martinsyde as was Emmet Dalton. Broy, like some ex-soldiers, used his experience from humble beginnings in the British security forces in Ireland. He had joined and resigned from the RIC within a three-week period in August 1910, later joining the Dublin Metropolitan Police in 1911. Later, as a trusted member of the "G" division, he became a double agent acting for Michael Collins during the War of Independence. He was arrested and imprisoned in Arbour Hill and after the Treaty was appointed by the Free State administration as secretary to the Department of Civil Aviation and then adjutant to the Free State Air Force.[278]

The first dozen or so pilots all had war experience. They were Jack McSweeney, Charlie Russell, James Fitzmaurice, Gerry Carroll, Bill Hannon, Fred Crossley, Tom Maloney, Bill Delamere, Bill McCullagh, Jack Flynn, Oscar Heron, Wilfred Hardy and Lt. Arnott.[279]

---

[277]Colonel Ned Broy, BMH, MA, WS 1280
[278]MacNiffe, p. 42
[279]Information kindly supplied by Mr A.T. Kearns: See also Donal MacCarron,
  A view from above: 200 years of aviation in Ireland (Dublin, 2000)

All of these pilots were ex-Royal Air Force but Lt. Arnott was later discovered to be a former Auxiliary and was subsequently thrown out of the force and the country at gunpoint.[280] Many of the rank and file also had previous British military experience, such as ex-RAF Sergeant Major O'Toole. Russell and O'Toole later miraculously survived a serious crash when the non-technical O'Toole inadvertently mismanaged the controls of the aircraft during a routine maintenance check. The first military aircraft purchased were a selection of surplus WWI types including Avro 504Ks, Bristol F2Bs, DH9s and Martinsyde Buzzards. General McSweeney delivered a Bristol Fighter BII the first aircraft brought by air from Croydon on 4 July. Almost immediately frequent reconnaissance and other missions were conducted in support of National Army troops on the ground against Republican forces. Although there was some action between Republicans and the aviators the first major engagement between an aircraft and enemy troops occurred on 3 December 1922.

The Irish Times elaborated on the incident:

'For the first time says our Cork correspondent, an aeroplane has been brought into action against bodies attacking national soldiers, with the result that in withdrawing after an ambush, an entire column was bombed from the air. The details of this sensational move, learned from official quarters here, are that a party of national troops was travelling between Drimoleague and Dunmanway, conducting operations in this wide area. About sixty fully equipped armed men sighted the military in two lorries and prepared to ambush them. They took up well-covered positions behind high fences on the roadside. When the lorries were passing intensive fire was opened on them. One soldier was killed. The troops replied with fire but realised that they were outnumbered and that their attackers were in excellent positions and sent for reinforcements. An aeroplane also came. It was of the small scouting type. The plane soon came up with the ambush party, locating them near a wood towards Leap. The pilot descended to a few hundred feet and when over the ambush party, nose dived in their direction.'[281]

---

[280]Ibid, p.57

[281]*The Irish Times,* 5 December. 1922

This, as one may remember, is the same region as some of the most successful and spectacular confrontations took place between flying columns and British forces during the Irish War of Independence only a few years previously. Although the National Army could not and did not utilise this conventional and modern resource effectively throughout the rest of the Civil War it still would have had some effect on the morale of the Republican forces in the field. Remember that this method of co-operation between land and air forces became quite effective by the time of the Second World War and is still very much in use today. The same report on the incident described how the aircraft, which was flown by Lt. J. C. Fitzmaurice (an ex-British serviceman) in dropping bombs and firing on the enemy force caused consternation and that the dramatic employment of aircraft against Republicans made a great impression in Cork.[282]

This was no doubt a brilliant opportunity for government propaganda and a republican rethink on field operations. McSweeney, Russell, Fitzmaurice, Carroll, Maloney and DeLamere all became Officers Commanding the Irish Army Air Corps.[283] Russell later took charge of the formation and training of the Railway Protection Corps while McSweeney was one of the Air Service officers who was involved in the Army Mutiny of 1924. These first thirteen pilots of the early Air Service developed the force and fought against Republican forces throughout the Civil War.[284]

---

[282]Ibid, see also Lt Col' Mick O' Malley, 'Modest beginnings in times of strife: the air service years', in *The Irish Air Corps 1922-1927* an official souvenir (Dublin, 1997), pp 6-9

[283]*Freeman's Journal*, 7 June. 1922 reported the arrival of an Avro aeroplane to be used in Baldonnel to train Irish airmen and the *Irish Times*, 5 Dec. 1922 reported the first offensive action of an aircraft

[284]For a military assessment on this organisation and army see Mulcahy papers, UCDA, P7/B/43, P7/B/47, P7/B/49; *Freeman's Journal*, 7 June. 1922; *Irish Times*, 5 Dec. 1922.

Fitzmaurice in particular had served as a foot soldier in the trenches.[285] He had joined the Volunteers prior to the war and had always been interested in things military. He admired the ex-British drill instructors but resented the role played by the officers. These were 'an inept lot of shopkeepers and such like, masquerading under the delusion that officers were produced by the tailors who made their uniforms. From a military point of view they were a pathetic lot of cretins who neither looked like, nor behaved like soldiers.'[286] With the outbreak of war he repeatedly tried to join the army against the wishes of his parents, as he was under age, but was ultimately successful when he commenced training as a member of the 17th Lancers. Fitzmaurice had been fascinated by the paradox of Irishmen fighting England's war.[287] 'The Irish were going to war in a cause propounded by their centuries old enemy. They were going to fight for the independence of small nations. Had they not won everybody's battles but their own?'[288]

By 1916 it was realised that cavalry in the strictest term would not have the traditional place it once held on the modern battlefield any more. Right up to the end of hostilities some, like General Douglas Haig, a cavalry officer by trade, still hoped and longed for the breakthrough in trench warfare that a traditional cavalry charge might exploit and in doing so break the deadlock. The need to replace manpower in depleted units at the front meant the cavalry units like the 17th Lancers would have to send its troopers into active service infantry battalions to build up their fighting strengths.

Fitzmaurice was in due course posted to an English fighting unit, the 7th Battalion of the Queen's Royal (West Surrey) Regiment, the Second Regiment of Foot and part of the 55th Brigade of the British 18th Division, which was fighting on the Somme.[289] One of the major

---

[285]Teddy Fennelly, *Fitz and the famous flight* (Portlaoise, 1997), pp. 36-61.
[286]Ibid, pp. 23-24
[287]Teddy Fennelly, *Fitz and the famous flight,* p.25
[288]Ibid
[289]Ibid pp. 36-37

actions that Fitzmaurice was to take part in as part of this unit was the attack on Thiepval on 26 September 1916. His Brigade, the 55th, was involved in the successful assault on the village and the formidable Schwaben Redoubt on 28 September. The casualties numbered 1,500 all ranks for Thiepval and 2,000 for Schwaben.[290]

On 6 January 1917, Fitzmaurice turned 19 years old, the official age for soldiers to serve overseas. He was however by this stage a seasoned combat soldier in charge of No. 13 Platoon of D Company of the 7th Queens and he was to see plenty more action. He received a wound to his leg in fighting during May of that year when after one particularly intense period in the line, only twenty one men answered the roll call from the 850 who originally went in.[291] Soon afterwards he was sent to train for promotion to a commissioned rank as an officer, later applying for pilot training and had just received his wings when the war ended. His superiors noticed his skill as a pilot and around that time he became the first man to do a night flight mail crossing of the channel.[292]

On return to Ireland in 1922 Fitzmaurice joined the Free State Army Air Force and conducted operations against Republican forces.[293] He became famous in 1928 as part of a crew of three in the successful first East-West non-stop trans-Atlantic flight between Ireland and the American continent, which took off from Baldonnel in a German Junkers aircraft known as the Bremen. This event helped Ireland to take on the mantle of romantic aviation.

Fitzmaurice's friend Lieutenant Thomas Joseph Maloney, later Commandant and officer commanding the Irish Air Service was born on 16 January 1899 at Shanagolden in County Limerick. He was educated at St. Peter's Freshfield and St. Manchin's College Limerick, Maguire's Civil Service College, Dublin and Birmingham University.

---

[290]Ibid, pp. 47-49

[291]Ibid p.57

[292]Ulick O' Connor, *Oliver St John Gogarty: A poet and his times*, (London, 1963), p.228

[293]Teddy Fennelly, *Fitz and the famous flight*

He had also harboured aspirations of crossing the Atlantic by air as early as 1924 in the Martinsyde or the "Big Fella" of Michael Collins fame as mentioned earlier but this did not transpire. However, after transferring from the Yorkshire Regiment, Maloney had a distinguished and extraordinarily long operational career (for a flying officer) of over eighteen months in the RAF during the war. He specialised in long range bombing of German positions on the Western front. After the war he returned to Ireland taking up a position as surveyor of taxes in the Inland Revenue Department. When the Civil War broke out, he joined the Free State Army in August 1922 and the new military air service where he served as a pilot in Baldonnel for three months. He was appointed as commanding officer at Fermoy from October 1922 to January 1923 and carried out operations during the conflict. Commandant Maloney became the third officer of the Free State Air Force to be killed when his aircraft struck a tree near the Curragh while on manoeuvres on 22 September 1925.[294]

The most notable wartime ace to join the Air Service was Oscar Heron who had served in France with No. 70 Squadron. He flew "Camel" aircraft and shot down two enemy aircraft on 30 June 1918 and two more Fokker DVIIIs a few weeks later helping him earn the Distinguished Flying Cross (DFC) with a total of nine enemy aircraft destroyed. By October, Heron had reached the rank of Flight Commander and received the Belgian Croix de Guerre. He served in the Irish Air Service until he was killed in the Phoenix Park in 1933 during an air display.[295] Dublin man Frederick Crossley, who had served with No. 1 Squadron Royal Flying Corps was another member of the early Irish Air Service. He had been injured while successfully shooting down a German 2-seater aircraft. The rear gunner of the enemy aircraft kept firing as he plummeted to the ground and one of

[294]*The Irish Times,* 23 September. 1925; *The Irish Times,* 25 September. 1925; *Irish Independent,* September 23, 1925

[295]Donal MacCarron, 'The first pilots' in *The Irish Air Corps 1922-1927* an official souvenir (Dublin, 1997), pp 10-11

his rounds came through the floor of Crossley's machine, clipping his clothing and, with its momentum reduced tunnelled up through his body and was finally stopped by his palate. Crossley had also been involved in an indecisive encounter with Baron von Richthofen (the Red Baron) as had another Irish Air Service pilot Jack Flynn. Flynn had been employed by the Irish Air Service in the instructional arena but rose quickly through the system to the rank of Commandant. This may have been as a result of his previous active record in the IRA against the Black and Tans during the War of Independence and post Great War service.[296]

Colonel William Percy Delamere or "Bill" to his friends was from Mullingar in Co. Westmeath and joined the Irish Air Service in September 1922, after previous war service with No.19 Squadron in France.[297] He had joined up at 16 years of age after leaving St. Mary's Christian Brothers School, Mullingar in 1915 to fight in the war. In January 1916 he joined the Officer Training Corps (OTC) and by December was a member of the RFC training with 49 Reserve Squadron and 54 Reserve/Training Squadron. He was commissioned on 5 April and awarded his wings on 1 June 1917, having completed three months at the school of Aeronautics in Oxford and courses on aerial gunnery at Tunbury. He also completed an instructor's course at Gosport and attended the School of Aerial Fighting at Spiral Gate. In September of that year he was posted to France to serve as Lieutenant with 19 Squadron RFC and on 21 October, his 18th birthday, he recorded his first experience over enemy lines. On 3 January 1918, Lt. Delamere was wounded in the leg during aerial combat and was hospitalised but by 25 August he was back flying again, in the newly formed RAF.

In December, 1918, Bill like many thousands more, was demobbed. He studied automotive engineering for a period and returned to Ireland to join the Irish Air Service on 21 September 1922 under the command of General McSweeney, arriving in Baldonnel as a Lieutenant.

---

[296]Ibid
[297]Ibid

By 22 November he was stationed in Fermoy and on 16 January 1923 at approximately 4 p.m. while flying a Bristol Fighter BI to Brendan's Glenn with his passenger, 2nd Lt. Flanagan, they came under fire from Irregulars on the ground. They returned fire and dropped two bombs. By October 1924, Bill had been promoted to Captain, in 1931 he was a member of the first Command and Staff course run by the Irish Defence Forces and in February 1939 was instructed, as commandant of the Air Corps School, to prepare plans for air defence. On 22 June 1940 he was appointed Officer Commanding Air Defence Command and on 24 March 1943, Director of Military Aviation and Officer Commanding the Irish Air Corps. Delamere was promoted to Colonel in March 1945 and later retired to Aer Rianta as first manager of Dublin Airport at the request of the Department of Industry and Commerce.[298]

The Irish Air Service became the Irish Air Corps in 1924 and though nearly all the pilots of the early Irish Air Service had seen British war service, the observers for the two-seater machines were predominately men from the Free State Army who had previous IRA service. At least one of them had been involved in the 1916 rising.[299] The British government had offered the use of RAF officers on reserve to train the Free State's air force or to carry out other duties with the proviso that they would be released in times of national mobilisation. It is unclear if this occurred although some of those who had already joined may have been on reserve to the British forces. This was the same throughout the army and reservists were usually discharged automatically when joining.[300]

---

[298]The dress uniform of Col' Delamere and a record of his military career are on display in the Officers Mess, Casement Aerodrome Baldonnel courtesy of his son Peter who gifted the collection. This information is supplied thanks to the Officers Mess of the Irish Air Corps Baldonnel

[299]MacCarron, 'The first pilots' in *The Irish Air Corps 1922-1927 an official souvenir* pp10-11

[300]Governor General files F.71, NAI, Colonial Office dispatch to Governor General Irish Free State 17 September 1925; Dept of Taoiseach papers NAI, Letter 10 Downing St to Provisional Government dated 28 December 1921 declaring no objection to reservists serving in national forces S3238, S/896

The dynamic of pre-Treaty IRA and ex-British servicemen serving together in the fledgling force must have caused rifts between those involved in the pre-Truce struggle and those who were involved in the Great War, especially amongst the officers.

There is one other interesting point to be introduced here regarding the fears of the Northern Ireland political hierarchy towards the capabilities of the Free State air force. Although the Civil War in the south was extremely beneficial to Unionist stability in the north they had a siege mentality even when there was no reason to do so. In the early months of the Civil War Major-General Solly-Flood, the Northern government's security advisor, was increasingly concerned about the threat that the southern government's air force posed.[301] The Free State air force was too meagre to pose such a threat never mind carry it out, but maybe it was good propaganda for loyalist concerns. It may have prompted the British authorities to carry out an intelligence survey of the aviation branch of the National Army. The actual intelligence report produced by the RAF in 1922 is quite derogatory towards the Free State Air Force and its personnel. It describes the officers as being young, inexperienced and of somewhat low order of intelligence and social standing. This is interesting because the personnel they spoke of were all experienced men who fought in the RAF with Great War experience. Russell and McSweeney also had republican credentials and were the two men who purchased and maintained an aircraft on British soil under the noses of the British military, while the Treaty negotiations were underway.[302] Maybe, just maybe, they had a point. The freedom fighter had been left in charge and it was a new ball game for those not accustomed to disciplinary constraints.[303]

---

[301]Michael Hopkinson, Civil War and aftermath 1922-4 in R. J. Hill, ed.,
  A new history of Ireland Vol. VII, *Ireland 1921-1984*, p.59
[302]This intelligence report is reproduced in part in Patrick J. McCarthy,
  The RAF and Ireland 1920-2 in *The Irish sword, The journal of the military
  history society of Ireland*, Vol. XVII, No 68 9Dublin, 1989), pp187-8
[303]Teddy Fennelly, *Fitz and the famous flight*, pp94-5

As Major Fitzmaurice of the Irish Air Service pointed out when describing what he observed in early 1922 on his appointment at Baldonnel.

'It was quite a change from the well trained, neatly uniformed and state-of-the–art arms and aircraft of the British Army and Royal Air Force to a newly formed air service with a few trained personnel, poor discipline, few aircraft and the most basic facilities… The officer commanding was an ex-cadet of the Royal Air Force whose flying experience was practically nil… this youth bore the exalted rank of Major General and was always accompanied by an equally youthful aide-de-camp, who was festooned with lethal weapons presenting a picture that resembled something out of a comic strip, an air of hedonism prevailed at the Aerodrome where the most amazing characters kept popping in and settling down, though they had nothing whatsoever to do with the organisation…some of them bore exalted ranks which they appear to have conferred upon themselves.. In cases they were almost completely illiterate.'[304]

For a professional like Fitzmaurice, the ad hoc military system in the early days must have undermined his confidence and place in the scheme of things but this would soon change.

Ex-British Soldiers and Legalisation of the Irish Army

By the end of 1922 the new army of the Irish Free State had survived the turbulent first year of independence. It now sought a transition from a semi-legal entity to an organisation encompassing a full legal and constitutional status and an establishment to distinguish it from its guerrilla roots.[305] A systematic model was needed for the legalisation of the army. In June 1922, Mr. Cahir Davitt, a circuit court judge, was asked by Michael Collins to become judge advocate general to the army. Davitt was under no illusions to the magnitude of the work and

---

[304]Ibid
[305]Patrick Long, p.316

established a legal section in the adjutant general's branch, which was responsible for the conduct of courts martial and general administration.[306] He recruited a group of ex-British officers as support staff to manage the section based in Portobello Barracks. This was done with the aid of George Hodnett, (a Major in the Great War), Theodore Cunningham Kingsmill Moore, (ex-RAF officer and defender of Trinity College in 1916, who had been tasked with drafting charge sheets and courts-martial procedures by General W.R.E. Murphy) and also John Donovan, Charlie Casey and Thomas Coyne. All were ex-army or RAF with extensive active service in France so it was inevitable that the British military system would dominate the new Irish military code.[307]

The general regulations as to discipline were promulgated as a general order and came into effect on 1 November 1922.[308] There were many technical problems but some defendants at courts-martial were affronted if British Army 'spit and polish' was lacking. In general discipline was good amongst ex-British servicemen.[309] But one case was that of an ex-British soldier who General O'Duffy reported to GHQ, charged with sodomy.[310] That was however a singular incident and by no means a regular occurrence. The General Regulations were based on the British Army's Manual of Military Law, which Davitt had purchased in Eason's bookstore. The later constituted Defence Forces (Temporary Provisions) Act 1923 was largely based on the British Army (Annual) Act and the Reserve Forces Act of 1889.[311] One might consider that this act was outdated by thirty years in 1923 but the army needed to solve the problem sooner rather than later. The British were

---

[306]Duggan, PP 115-137.

[307]Ibid.

[308]Ibid.

[309]Ibid; See also Mulcahy papers, UCDA, P7/B/56, memoranda on penal code in British military law

[310]O'Duffy papers, UCDA, P24/222, General O' Duffy to executive council 12 June 1924; McGarry, p.137.

[311]Ibid.

also revamping their system after the world war. Thirty years is not a long time but the war outdated many military tactics and laws. It is interesting also that the modern Irish Defence Forces have only relatively recently begun to upgrade its military acts some of which were instituted in the mid 1950s and earlier, a gap of fifty years.

Attitudes & Allegiances

During the Civil War, Republicans and soldiers of the Irregular forces and many on the government side were incensed towards ex-British servicemen serving in the army, even if they were Irishmen. The Irregulars felt they were fighting the old enemy in the form of the Irish Free State government and army. This can be gauged at a minor level by the attitudes towards the National Army and ex-servicemen from those on the Republican bench. This is interesting as some in the British hierarchy held quite similar views to the Republicans about the army and the inclusion of ex-British soldiers, especially in the IRA, albeit in a different context. On 9 May 1922, the British secretary of state for war was asked 'if his Majesty would deprive officers of honorary rank or decoration for gallant service who have joined the rebel army in Ireland to take up arms against the forces of the Crown.'[312]

Generally people were not sure what was going on and this led to propaganda frenzy on both sides that used the existence of ex-British soldiers in the army and their oath of allegiance very effectively. Some in the British government were unsure as to who was funding the Civil War. A question was asked in the House of Commons 'if the British taxpayer was paying for the Free State troops.'[313]

---

[312]The parliamentary debates, fifth series, House of Commons, 10 April - May 12 1922, (vol. 153) (London, 1922), p.1979.

[313]The Parliamentary Debates, fifth series, House of Commons, 20 November - 25 December 1922 (vol. 159), (London, 1923), p.1487.

In July 1922 Frank Aiken, commanding the 4th Northern Division IRA, outlined the position of his forces with reference to the Treaty and National Army when he asked his men:

> ' . . . for the country's sake not to join the army of the government with that oath in the constitution, no matter what the pay may be or the alternatives to joining are starving or going back to Ulster at a time that the disordered state of Southern Ireland ensures failure . . . '[314]

Republicans saw the new army and government as being complicit with the British. The taking of an oath of allegiance to the Crown merely justified this view. On 13 April 1922 members of the IRA's No. 1 Dublin brigade and members of Tipperary units took over the Four Courts in Dublin, the centre of the country's legal system. Proclaiming it as the Republican military headquarters, Rory O'Connor, Liam Mellows and Ernie O'Malley wanted to force the Provisional Government to submit. Tom Barry and others later joined them. After the National Army attack on the Four Courts, which triggered the outbreak of the Civil War, anti-Treaty propaganda denounced the government. Republican propagandists exaggerated the number and role of ex-British officers in the army representing it as a green clad regiment of the British Army; they could have had no exact idea as to the amount of veterans who had joined. However, the army had one huge advantage over the British forces of two years earlier, it was Irish and shared with the IRA the local knowledge that the British had lost once the RIC had been paralysed.[315]

There were divergent attitudes towards ex–servicemen, for instance on 9 May 1922, the Freeman's Journal reported the repatriation to Ireland of the remains of 64 Irish-born American soldiers, killed in France in the war.[316] Those soldiers had been Irishmen serving a foreign state for

[314]Frank Aiken papers, UCDA, P104/1247(4),
[315]Garvin, The birth of Irish democracy, p.125
[316]Freeman's Journal, 9 May, 1922

some of the same ideals and reasons as men who joined the British forces at the same time. They had left their families in the hope of changing their conditions. They fought in the hope of surviving the daily claim of death from every corner in the carnage of that conflict; they were considered heroes, as were soldiers in other countries.

In contrast, the government soldiers were believed by Republicans to belong to the same underclass of ex-British servicemen, which they had derided on their return from the war. They were the victims of the same scorn as they shared all the vices, 'fella's not working, hanging around and hangers-on who'd been through the 14-18 war.'[317] The majority of those ex-soldiers, who were the corner-boys and loafers of the towns a few months ago, had brought their corner-boy propensities with them into the army and drunkenness and indiscipline were the order of the day.[318] Peter Hart described this for Mallow 'where they have now got the worst type of ex-soldier in the Free State Army, while in Kerry the IRA's foes were the drunkard, the traitor, the wife deserter, wife beater, the tramp, the tinker and the brute.'[319] Many soldiers returned from the front physically injured, mentally scarred or haunted by their experiences. It may have been better if none had returned alive as the scorn set against them certainly didn't give much hope that their sacrifices and troubles were enough to change society for the better or to at least receive an honoured welcome home.

Is it not strange that the IRA could say these things and yet use ex-soldiers themselves? During the National Army's advance into Tralee, the effective fire of at least three ex-British soldiers working as snipers for the anti-Treaty forces in the area held up its progress for a considerable period of time.

---

[317]O' Malley papers, UCDA, P17a/34, Intelligence reports, n.d.1922;
Hart, *The IRA and its enemies,* p.149.
[318]Hart, *The IRA and its enemies,* p.149
[319]Ibid

Earlier during the War of Independence another ex-soldier, Con Healy who was a crack marksman of A Company 1st Battalion IRA, was tasked with shooting the notorious Auxiliary officer, Major McKinnon, on the Tralee golf course in 1921.[320]

Appearance, demeanour and accent of ex-servicemen, especially former British officers, also affected the attitudes of Republicans and some within the Free State Army towards these men. The gentleman's aloofness and educated class distinctions fomented within the British military officer corps and public school system was still borne by some of these men new to the Irish Army. This would have had those with anti-English sentiments seething with rage and cut deeply those IRA officers in the force. This must have hurt even more so as the hierarchal officer corps and enlisted establishments of the Free State Army were built upon the British model and this was reflected in the Irish military routine and system until quite recently.

The Great War had also given the middle classes in England an opportunity to prove themselves in the officer corps, much to the consternation of the professional officers of the army. This was reflected in Ireland too. The feudal type of advancement in the British model was exactly the type of fundamental symbol of the Empire and British-ness that many had originally sought to remove by fighting for the Republic. To some, the fact that ex-British officers were holding senior positions in the army must have resembled a situation where peasants were being lead by the landed gentry again. This type of scenario also helped to fuel comparisons of the new government and army with that of the old establishment and was useful in anti-Treaty propaganda towards the now established military forces of the new Irish state. The Four Courts defenders issued a statement, which called upon 'our former comrades of the Irish Republic to return to that allegiance and thus guard the nation's honour from the infamous stigma that her sons aided her foes in returning a hateful dominion over

---

[320]Harrington, p. 37

her'.[321] It also brought forward the 'spirit of the illustrious dead' who were with them in this great struggle.[322] The taking of a British institution with British shells turned on fellow Irishmen gave them another symbolic victory.[323]

Some of the more political Civil War propaganda aimed at the pro-Treaty side was published in *Poblacht na hÉireann,* War News, on 30 June 1922 and was probably produced by Erskine Childers, an ex-soldier, secretary to the Treaty delegates in London and now the Republican propaganda chief.

It read:

'RALLY TO THE FLAG
IT'S A WAR

WHO BEGAN THE WAR? HIS MAJESTY'S FREE STATE MINISTERS
WHO ARE THEY ATTACKING? THEIR OWN BROTHER IRISHMEN
OF THE IRISH REPUBLICAN ARMY
WHY DID THEY BEGIN THE ATTACK? BECAUSE LLOYD GEORGE
AND CHURCHILL TOLD THEM THEY MUST
WHO ARE THEIR ALLIES IN THE WAR? THE ENGLISH
WHAT ARE THEIR WEAPONS IN THE WAR? ARTILLARY,
MACHINEGUNS, RIFLES ETC SUPPLIED BY THE ENGLISH
WHAT IS THEIR OBJECT IN THE WAR? TO DESTROY THE IRISH
REPUBLIC AND MAKE YOU SWEAR ALLEGIENCE TO THE KING
OF ENGLAND AS KING OF IRELAND.

**PEOPLE OF IRELAND, WHICH SIDE ARE YOU ON IN THE WAR,
THERE CAN BE ONLY ONE ANSWER YOU ARE ON THE SIDE
OF IRELAND.**

WE HEAR ON THE BEST AUTHORITY THAT GENERAL Mc
CREADY IS WITH THE PROVISIONAL GOVERNMENT ADVISING
ON THE WAR'[324]

---

[321]Purdon, p.36
[322]Ibid
[323]Ibid
[324]*Poblacht na hEireann* War News, 30 June. 1922

General Dalton, Director of Military Operations at this stage is said to have urged the use of artillery on the Four-Courts as the use of these guns would have been quite demoralising upon a garrison unused to artillery fire. He was speaking from his own wartime experience.[325] The government, in response to allegations that they had used British military forces during the attack, addressed Republican propaganda in the Freeman's Journal on 1 July 1922

'MESSAGE TO THE NATIONAL FIGHTING FORCES FROM GOVERNMENT OF IRELAND

"False and malicious statements have been made against you. It has been said that British troops have cooperated with you'[326]

The Irish Times carried another reply on 3 July 1922; this time in the form of an official bulletin issued the previous evening from GHQ concerning the men who worked the guns at the Four Courts. It reads,

> *'In view of the fact that fictitious stories are being circulated, it is necessary to state that the artillery used against the Four Courts was under the command of Major General Dalton, who, it will be remembered, entered Mountjoy Prison in an attempt to rescue Major General Sean McEoin last year'.*[327]

Pressure had been brought to bear on the Irish government by the British cabinet after IRA volunteers in London assassinated Field-Marshall Sir Henry Wilson, military advisor to the six county administration.[328] Winston Churchill warned that the Treaty would be regarded as being violated if the Four Courts were not cleared. The British blamed the garrison there for Wilson's murder. The artillery guns used to open fire on the Four Courts signalling the beginning of

[325]Younger, p.321
[326]*Freeman's Journal*, 1 July. 1922
[327]*The Irish Times*, 3 July, 1922
[328]Wilson was assassinated on 22 June 1922 near his London home

the Civil War had in fact come from the British Army. Winston Churchill had provided the weapons and the delivery was carried out under the co-operation of General McCready, Commander of British forces still in Ireland.

General Emmet Dalton who was in command of the military operations in Dublin, summoned General A.T. Lawlor an ex-soldier from Athlone, with a hastily assembled crew. He had been trying to instruct them in the use of a gun which was an old horse artillery piece that had been left in the barracks. On the night of 27 June 1922 the British Army transferred a number of eighteen-pounder artillery guns to the Irish Free State Army in the Phoenix Park Dublin, not far from the Four Courts.[329] Supplied with only ten rounds of shrapnel per gun they opened fire on the anti-Treaty position at 4 am on 28 June, crossing a point of no return that has gone down in the annals of Irish history.[330] Carlton Younger tells us that, 'Emmet Dalton and Tony Lawler directed the artillery gunfire on the Four-Courts with the professional detachment of men who had gone through the hell flames of France.'[331]

The Provisional Government had to be extremely careful about assistance from the British, as this would also deliver a propaganda victory to the anti-Treaty side and might influence national and international opinion. As it turned out, propaganda was used intensely throughout the conflict by both sides, with the government flexing its muscles on the official press. Early in October it issued instructions to newspapers and the media as regards the reporting of incidents to do with the conflict. In future the army was to be referred to as the

[329]Florence O'Donoghue papers c.1912-16, NLI, Ms, 31,260 copy of letter from Frank Carney ex O/C 1st Northern Division Derry to E Donnelly Director of Elections re arms requested from British for attack on Four Courts 14 Nov 1924; The guns came from Marlborough barracks, now McKee barracks Dublin

[330]Morrison, p.75

[331]Younger, p.327

'national army', Irish army, or just 'troops', the Irregulars were not to be described as either 'forces' or 'troops' nor were their leaders to be given their ranks; and the words 'Republicans', 'attacked', 'commandeered', and 'arrested' were to be replaced by 'Irregulars', 'fired at', 'seized' and 'kidnapped' respectively.[332]

Erskine Childers had been very instrumental in arming the Volunteers prior to 1916 using his boat the *Asgard,* which he sailed from America loaded with rifles. He was a former Clerk of the House of Commons Committees, secretary of Lloyd George's Irish Convention of 1917, which sought agreement on the Home Rule Bill. Elected to represent Wicklow in the Dáil in 1921 he later became its Director of Propaganda and Publicity and during the Treaty talks was secretary to the plenipotentiaries.[333] Childers had seen service in the Boar War and after 1916 he again served in the Royal Navy. After the war he returned to his Republican ideals and during the Civil War ran a prolific anti-Free State propaganda operation and was involved in the Dublin fighting. He was later captured, court-martialled and shot by government forces during the Civil War, for the unlawful possession of a pistol, which Michael Collins had earlier presented to him. He was shot while awaiting the result of an appeal. Cosgrave and his colleagues did not want to make an exception of him as they agreed that Childers had made some inflammatory and misleading statements during the Treaty debates, which were perceived to provoke many of those who took up arms against the Treaty.[334] His own Anglo-Irish roots were indeed used against him by those on the Free State side to pass moral judgement and question his ideals and loyalty to Ireland. Even his accent was against him; he was regarded as 'that damned English spy'. Winston Churchill was to say of him on learning of his capture that he had,

[332]Purdon, pp48-9
[333]Duggan, p. 102; O'Farrell, p.15.
[334]Risteard Mulcahy, *Richard Mulcahy 1886-1971: A family memoir* (Dublin, 1999), p.195

'seen with satisfaction that the mischief-making murderous renegade, Erskine Childers, has been captured. No man has done more harm or shown more genuine malice or endeavoured to bring a greater curse upon the common people of Ireland than this strange being'.

Childers, the British ex-soldier had carried out his role in the Republican movement very effectively and as a result was feared. This further emphasises how unclear, slanderous and blurred the politics of the period was. *The Freeman's Journal* on 25 April 1922 carried this article,

'There can be but one opinion of Childers's attempt to exalt his superior republican virtue by hurling scurrilities from his paper at all Irishmen, by flinging mud at men who were risking their lives for this country while he was parading in a British uniform. There is no honest man, whatever his political views may be, who will not feel a spasm of disgust when he finds Mr. Childers, the ex-British yeoman, asserting that Michael Collins by marvellous luck, secured a wonderful rebel attack upon himself. He insults not only Irish readers but Ireland itself. Mr. Childers may trick himself out with green white and yellow trappings but when his real voice is heard it is indistinguishable from that of the diehards of the Morning Post.' [335]

Childers, Robert Barton and David Robinson were some of those Anglo-Irish ex-soldiers who took the Republican side after the treaty. Robinson was to continually suffer due to his wartime experiences in Europe. Prior to his role as adjutant to a short-lived cavalry company raised in the South he had been a major in the British Tank Corps and severely wounded while fighting in France.[336] Barton, who was from Wicklow, was a cousin of Erskine Childers and had served in the

---

[335]*The Freeman's Journal,* 25 April, 1922
[336]O'Malley, The singing flame, pp 203-04

British Army, he guarded prisoners during the 1916 Rebellion. He resigned his commission soon afterwards and joined the Irish Volunteers reaching the rank of Commandant. In 1918 he was elected for West Wicklow and Kildare and was present at the First Dáil in January 1919. Arrested on more than one occasion for making seditious speeches he was sentenced and later escaped from Mountjoy Prison. Appointed Minister for Agriculture in April 1919 he later instigated the Land Bank Schemes and afterwards became Minister for Economic Affairs, a member of the Truce Observation Committee and he was Treaty negotiator and signatory.[337]

Robinson was arrested with Childers by the Free State Army while on active service in the Cork and Kerry areas and spent time in Mountjoy and Kilmainham, where he was jail adjutant.[338] But Childers was the great prize.

On 15 October 1922 the Dáil had issued an order announcing an amnesty for all who were willing to lay down their arms 'in the present state of armed rebellion and insurrection'. The Dáil also gave the army council special powers to try in military courts and punish anyone who was in breach of the regulation and Childers became one of the first of seventy-seven victims. The offences were punishable by fine, internment, imprisonment, penal servitude and death according to the offence. Other offences included

> 'taking part in or aiding and abetting any attacks upon the national forces; looting, arson and other damage to public or private property and most significantly in the possession of any bomb, or any articles in the nature of a bomb, or any dynamite, gelignite, or other explosive substance, or any revolver, rifle, gun or other firearm or lethal weapon or any ammunition for such firearm'.

---

[337]Padraig O' Farrell, *Who's who in the Irish War of Independence and Civil War 1916-1923*, (Dublin, 1997), p.6

[338]Ibid, p. 191

Of the fifteen men selected to execute him only five had loaded rifles. It had been pre-arranged that the five soldiers with loaded rifles were ex-Great War soldiers, apparently because of their superior marksmanship. Hence his death was instantaneous and the 'marksmanship very accurate.'[339]

Earlier in June 1922 Viscount Curzon asked the secretary for the colonies how many British subjects had been murdered or died of wounds in Ireland since the signing of the Treaty. He was told that from 6 December, 15 RIC, 8 ex-RIC, 8 soldiers and 3 ex-soldiers and 15 civilians had died.[340] This was only the beginning and he was probably unaware of the scale of murder and intimidation that was still happening in the country against ex-British servicemen and the establishment. For instance, on 15 May 1922 the Freeman's Journal reported the 'shooting dead of a young British soldier in Batchelor's Walk, Dublin.'[341] On 18 May, British troops evacuated Portobello Barracks, Dublin.[342] On 22 June John Lawless, an ex-British Soldier, was dragged from his bed on Rutland Street in Dublin and shot in front of his wife.[343] On the same day two IRA men shot Field Marshall Sir Henry Wilson in London. Wilson had figured largely in the Curragh mutiny of 1912 and as security advisor to the Northern Ireland government was held responsible for the Ulster pogroms. Both of his killers, Joseph O'Sullivan and Reginald Dunne, the second in command of the London IRA, were ex-British soldiers. Their escape was hampered as one had a prosthetic leg as a result of the war. They were caught and later hanged on 10 August 1922.[344]

---

[339]Mulcahy, p.196, Childers was shot on 24 November 1922 after shaking hands with the members of the firing squad

[340]Curzon to secretary of state, *The parliamentary debates,* fifth series, *House of Commons,* 12 June-30 June 1922, (vol.155), (His Majesty's Stationary Office London, 1922), p.1664

[341]*Freeman's Journal,* 15 May. 1922

[342]*Freeman's Journal,* 18 May. 1922

[343]*Freeman's Journal,* 1 July. 1922

[344]Peter Cottrell, 'The Anglo-Irish War: the troubles of 1913-1922' in *Osprey essential histories series* (Oxford, 2006), p.85

In July Private Rogers (RAF), and Privates Baker and Sutherland were fired upon and wounded in Amiens Street, with Rogers succumbing to his wounds.[345] On 3 July the Freeman's Journal reported 'the false accusations and lies that "British Tommie's" were operating with the army.'[346] In the same month at Wallingford England, Thomas Edwin Ramsey, an ex-British soldier, was charged with inciting a private to steal revolvers for shipment to Ireland and another 'Catholic' ex-soldier was flogged in Belfast Gaol.[347] In December a British officer was kidnapped and the body of James Cleary was found in Tipperary with a note saying he had been shot as 'a convicted spy,' 'spies and traitors beware the first of many.'[348]

On 18 December Brian Bradley, a Catholic ex-British soldier with three years service, was taken from his home and shot by unknown men.[349] Pierce Murphy was shot in Waterford, on 1 January 1923 by uniformed men in dress similar to the National Army.[350] In Adamstown Wexford, in March of that year, Lieutenant Thomas Jones, Sergeant Edward Gorman and Volunteer Patrick Horan, all ex-British soldiers, were lured to their deaths, which were delivered in a truly despicable fashion. While searching for a missing soldier they were captured after a short gunfight. They were marched for a considerable distance before being put up against a wall and machine-gunned to death. Jones was severely beaten before being shot and was found to have twenty bullets in his body.[351] These men were shot with Tommy Guns, an automatic weapon capable of a high volume of fire and preferred by U.S. gangsters at the time and used by the IRA. Another soldier who was

---

[345]*Freeman's Journal*, 3 July. 1922
[346]Ibid
[347]*Freeman's Journal*, 10 July. 1922
[348]*Irish Times*, 7 Dec. 1922
[349]*Irish Times*, 18 Dec. 1922
[350]*Irish Times*, 3 Jan. 1923
[351]Mulcahy papers, UCDA, P7/A/22; *The Free Press*, 13 Mar. 1923

wounded in the earlier fight who had no previous military experience was given aid by the attackers.[352] The officer's family believed he was singled out because of his prior British Army service.[353]

The 'getting them at last' element of Republican vengeance still rang true during the Civil War but compare to this the role of British soldiers in the IRA. For instance, there is the case of Reginald Hathaway who, while serving with his regiment in Tralee, deserted to the IRA and took the anti-Treaty side during the conflict. He was captured in arms with two other volunteers and all three were executed by firing squad in Ballymullen barracks, Tralee, on 25 April 1923. Although he deserted he was still a British soldier and therefore on that army's wanted/missing list.[354] He was shot for attacking and killing government troops, some of whom were most likely ex-servicemen also.

Some ex-servicemen helped the IRA clandestinely during the war with the British, while working within the military sphere and as a result were still sometimes persecuted by others within the republican movement who did not know of the cooperation, even though they were in the same units and areas. With the discovery of former Auxiliaries in the ranks of the army and Air Corps, all who had previously held commissions in the British forces were treated with distrust by some politicians and most old IRA officers. Some British Army veterans serving in the National Army were accused of being ex-Black and Tans or Auxiliaries through the Republican propaganda machine or in local circles. These accusations had their desired effect and were left to hang, without any real proof, over the heads and performance of the accused. In one particular case Major James Fitzmaurice of the Free State Air Force spent much time proving his whereabouts so as to disprove the accusations by an officer and NCO

---

[352]*The Free Press,* 13 March, 1923
[353]Ibid
[354]Harrington, p.37

who had served under him. They swore witness to his role in the burning of Balbriggan by the Black and Tans when he was a British soldier in 1920. There was a concerted campaign within the army to gather intelligence on the background of former British officers to expose those who had helped the British military establishment in Ireland during the Black and Tan period. Fitzmaurice said, 'In the estimation of these morons Irish history commenced in 1916 and the rewards of office and employment were the special prerogative of these zealots, their relatives and friends.'[355]

In the beginning, those of the IRA who split to take sides during the war felt a natural disinclination to risk taking the lives of their old friends and comrades whom they found in opposition.[356] However, after the passing of the Public Safety Bill and when the official executions were carried out by the government this dynamic changed. They did not want to fight and kill former friends but maybe it was okay to kill those who had no connection with the previous struggle. Ex-servicemen who now served the government were a 'justifiable target' as they had no connection to the IRA and were oath bound to the old enemy.

It had become 'increasingly clear' to some, by as early as mid 1922 'that the Irregulars cannot hope to offer successful military resistance to the National army. Their operations are assuming more distinctly the character of a war upon the economic life of the Irish people.'[357]

---

[355]Teddy Fennelly, Fitz and the famous flight, p.116

[356]Michael Hopkinson, Civil War and aftermath in A new history of Ireland Vol. VII, p. 37

[357]Department of Taoiseach papers, NAI, S1602, S1342, printed notice July 1922
from Minister of Local Government, Post and Telegraphs communications with Postmaster General 21 July – 6 September 1922

At the beginning of the conflict the Irregulars had a majority of trained men and weapons but this disproportion was dealt with by intensive recruiting into the National Army and a steady supply of weapons and ammunition, including artillery pieces from the British. By the end of the war Britain had provided £1 million worth of arms and supplies to the Free State.[358] In military terms, the Free State Army and not its opponents had displayed almost all the skill and energy.[359] Unlike the IRA during the Tan War, who had a much greater amount of local autonomy and less control by Sinn Féin, the new army obeyed its central controlling element in the form of the government and its head quarters in Dublin.

The lead into conflict had been slow and extremely complicated but in the end it was actually quite a brief war, lasting less than twelve months. However it has lived long in the collective memory of the Irish people. Beginning with severe fighting in the early phases as government troops tried to secure major towns, they were gradually forced into a guerrilla war with ambushes and reprisals. As the Civil War progressed cruelties took place on both sides and escalated with reprisals, murders, executions and atrocities with many high-ranking individuals falling victim. On 10 April 1923, Liam Lynch, who was by that time in command of Irregular forces, was mortally wounded in an engagement in the Knockmealdown Mountains while being pursued by government troops. Frank Aiken, who replaced him as chief of staff, declared a ceasefire on 30 April realising that any continuation of the struggle was folly. On 24 May he ordered anti-Treaty forces in the field to 'dump arms'. This call to give up the struggle included a message to the 'soldiers of the Republic, legion of the rearguard' by Eamon de Valera:

---

[358]Purdon, p. 39
[359]Laffen, p. 411.

'The republic can no longer be defended successfully by your arms. Further sacrifice of life would now be in vain and continuance of the struggle in arms unwise in the national interest and prejudicial to the future of our cause. Military victory must be allowed to rest with those who have destroyed the republic. Other means must be sought to safeguard the nation's right . . . much that you set out to accomplish is achieved . . . the people, exhausted by seven years of intense effort would rally again to the standard . . . when they are ready, you will be, and your place will be again as of old with the vanguard . . .'

National forces bombing the Hammam Hotel, 1922.
South Dublin Local Studies Collection.

'the only oath that concerned him was that oath of allegiance to the Dáil and as long as every member of the army kept that oath of allegiance, which he must take when he enters it, then he, Mr Brugha was satisfied'

Dáil Debates 1921

Chapter IV

AFTERMATH:

MUTINY, REMEMBRANCE AND COMMEMMORATION

OF THE IRISH CIVIL WAR

Remembrance of the First World War in the new Irish Free State was focused on a commemoration every year on the annual November services. These remembrance services were held in Dublin and other towns and locations throughout the country in the early years of the post war period and at least up to the early 1940s. The services were attended by thousands of people in the towns and in Dublin in particular, where the famous Ginchy cross was temporarily erected and acted as an Irish cenotaph. At 11 a.m. a two-minute silence was observed throughout the city. At the 1925 ceremony *The Irish Times* claimed that 120,000 people gathered in College Green. At the same remembrance ceremonies counter-demonstrations had been organised by Sinn Féin supporters and a smoke bomb was detonated in the crowd.[360]

---

[360]Author unknown, Ireland & the War: Early Remembrance and Revival, available at http://www.4eremdw.html [9 November, 2005]

On the Sunday before Remembrance Day hundreds of veterans would gather at sites around the city and, led by a band, they would parade in the morning through the streets of Dublin from Eden Quay to requiem mass at the Pro-Cathedral and in the afternoon to a service in St Patrick's cathedral. The Lord Mayor of Dublin and foreign ministers accredited to the Irish Free State attended those services. The yearly occurrence of disruption and violence in the centre of Dublin on remembrance weekend led to the ceremony being moved from the city centre to the Duke of Wellington monument in the Phoenix Park. There the Ginchy cross was once again erected and every year thousands of veterans and family members of men who had died would march up the quays along the River Liffey to the ceremony in the park. Widows wore their husband's medals and children would be seen wearing their father's medals. However, much to the disapproval of many of the veterans the conclusion of the service was signalled by the recital of the British national anthem. The act of remembrance had become politicised especially when Union Jack flags were being produced within sections of the crowd. It became difficult for certain elements in Irish society to distinguish between ex-servicemen commemorating their dead comrades and imperial factions exploiting the dead by turning the events into a political statement.

The existence of ex-British servicemen in the army had always been a bone of contention to some in Ireland, at least since 1916. The perceived alienation of some IRA veterans and their attitude to the treatment of ex-British servicemen in the Free State, also their existence in the army during the Irish Civil War and afterwards was used as one of the main excuses given by disgruntled 'Old IRA' officers for the army mutiny of 1924. For a long period after the First World War many ex-British servicemen also felt alienated. By the mid 1920s more than 100,000 Great War veterans had returned as civilians to Ireland. In 1928, 150,000 ex-British soldiers were resident in the Irish Free State.[361] In 1932 a list of veterans compiled for the British

[361]*Daily Press,* 12 Dec. 1927; Dept of Justice files Jus 8 NAI, Committee on claims of British ex-servicemen 1927-28

Legion in the area of Enniscorthy and district in Wexford revealed that 86 percent of ex-soldiers were occupied as 'labourers'.[362] These were working class men, non-agricultural workers, not well educated and in the early days unemployed, as was the case in many parts of the Free State. Many could not settle back into their lives in Ireland and some, with other ex-members of the RIC, began to emigrate to the colonies of the British Empire, helped of course by the British government.[364] After the RIC was disbanded in 1922 some of its officers moved to the Palestinian Gendarmerie and other colonial police forces. A total of 1,347 left the Free State and migrated to Northern Ireland, fearing for their position in the new state and hoping for new opportunities within the Empire.[364] By the mid 1920s, 483 of the 734 officers and men of the Palestine Gendarmerie were RIC veterans.[365] The Irish government was in no hurry to pay for their travel and it was unclear who should pay for their medical bills and resettlement.[366]

The Federation of Anglo-Irish War Victims was set up to lobby the governments for assistance and compensation for British subjects in Ireland for loss of life and property incurred during the troubles. These would have been RIC and civilian victims, probably a large proportion of landowners, Anglo-Irish victims of republican vandalism.[367]

---

[362]Pauline Codd, 'Recruiting and responses to the war in Wexford' in *Ireland and the First World War: the trinity history workshop*, (Dublin, 1986), p.15

[363]Resettlement to colonies i.e. Australia of ex-servicemen and ex-RIC, *The parliamentary debates*, fifth series, *House of Commons* 28 Mar. 1922 - 7 Apr. 1922 (vol.152), (His Majesty's Stationary Office London, 1923), p.1158.

[364]Alvin Jackson, Ireland, 'the union and the Empire 1800-1960', in Kevin Kenny, ed., *Ireland and the British Empire: Oxford history of the British Empire companion series*, p. 145

[365]Ibid

[366]Irish sailors and soldiers land trust established under section 3 of the Irish Free State (Consequential Provisions) Act 1922 for the purpose of carrying into effect the provisions of section 4 of the above act 1919, *Parliamentary debates, Dail Eireann*, 6 Dec. 1922 - 27 Mar. 1922 (Dublin Stationary Office, 1923), p. 1082.

[367] MP, UCDA, P7/B/395, P7/B/396

In 1927 the Committee on Claims of British ex-servicemen was set up at 5 Ely Place Dublin to lobby for those Irishmen who fought in the Great War. A public notice inviting evidence from organisations of British ex-servicemen was inserted in the press.[368] The committee had assistance from the British Legion, Department of Local Government, Public Health, Land Commission, the Irish Sailors and Soldiers Trust and The Organisation of British Ex-Servicemen.[369] There were some claims from men in respect of service in the National Army who had also served in the British forces but these were dismissed as not being in the terms of reference of the board.[370] In some cases soldiers who had been involved in the Connacht Rangers mutiny in India successfully claimed state assistance and pensions for service to Ireland.[371]

Loyalty, Faith and Honour

An Irish Times editorial on January 9 1922 sheds some insight into a discussion in the Dáil about the loyalties of ex-British soldiers to the new state.[372] Deputy Sean McGarry asked Mr Cathal Brugha, Minister for Defence, what he would say to an ex-member of the British army about his oath to England if he was about to join the Irish army.[373] His reply was 'that the only oath that concerned him was that oath of allegiance to the Dáil and as long as every member of the army kept that oath of allegiance, which he must take when he enters it, then he, Mr. Brugha was satisfied'.[374] This oath must have been a bone of

---

[368] Daily Press, 12 Dec. 1927; Dept of An Taoiseach S. files S.560, NAI, its members were Mr Cecil Lavery KG, Brigadier General R. Browne Clayton, Mr P.F. Baxter and Mr M.J. Beary of the Dept of Finance

[369] Ibid; Dept of An Taoiseach files, NAI, they wanted training and education for veterans and state assistance, education S4724, training S.4724 S.9701 S.10451 state assistance S.983

[370] Ibid.

[371] BMH, NAI, WS 1221 John Flannery participated in Connaught Rangers mutiny in India 1921

[372] Irish Times, 9 Jan. 1922

[373] Ibid

[374] Ibid

contention to many on both sides in the Civil War when it came to recruitment of ex-British soldiers. After all, those soldiers were seen as the old enemy. Disparaging references to 'mercenaries' and ex-British soldiers seemed to imply that their loyalty was in doubt, especially when measured against the purely voluntary anti-Treaty soldiers. Peter Young again makes the point that,

'As this was the first paid, full time Irish Army to be put in the field, there was cause to be suspicious of its loyalty. However, in the event, the vast majority remained loyal to the state.'[375]

However, this suspicion did not stop many ex-British soldiers changing allegiance from the Crown to a sworn loyalty to the new Free State coupled with the new oath to the king, although at the same time British soldiers were still being murdered. For instance, three officers and a soldier were murdered in Macroom in June that year, and as a result of the threat to soldiers a request was made to allow British officers to carry arms in the Free State.[376] This was during the British evacuation period when the military would have been at its most vulnerable.

When the Civil War commenced the anti-Treaty side continued to fight a guerrilla war while the army at first tried to fight the last war all over again in the British fashion of 1919-1921. Later they took a more conventional posture incorporating the lessons learnt by the IRA in order to fight the IRA.[377] The planning, training, logistics, officer ship and general ship of ex-British officers in the army would have brought a different kind of edge. For instance, the army had been reorganised

---

[375]Peter Young, *An Cosantoir review*, p. 141

[376]Dept of *Taoiseach* files, NAI, S.2087; The Parliamentary debates, fifth series, HC 12-30 June 1922 (vol. 155) His Majesty's stationary office 1922), pp 3556-7; Dept of *Taoiseach* files, NAI, S.2967, Compensation of death or injury of members of British forces in breach of Truce 10 Jan. 1923-19 Apr. 1925

[377]Paul V. Walsh, *'The Irish Civil War 1922-1924: A military study of the conventional phase 28 June-11 August 1922.'*

on British lines and although it came nowhere near to resembling the latter in terms of magnitude, those used to its structure and doctrine would have been able to maximise their military skills to the benefit of the formations they were now in control of.[378]

General Emmett Dalton, as mentioned earlier, was commander of government forces in the Cork area and had been an officer in the British Army.[379] He had served in Europe throughout the First World War with distinction rising up through the ranks to major and served with the Royal Dublin Fusiliers. He won the Military Cross at the Battle of Guinchy (from which he received his nickname) and was now a very important member of the Irish army hierarchy and he was also very close to Michael Collins, the Commander in Chief. He was Director of Training and later Director of Military Operations for the army during the Civil War and had already accompanied the plenipotentiaries to England during the Treaty talks.[380] He had also been involved in the War of Independence. There were many other officers like him in the armed forces who used their military expertise, learnt in the British military system, to further the aims of the government and military alike.[381] The NCOs and soldiers did the same and also trained and adopted aspects of the army into a disciplined entity in many areas. The professional conduct, conventionalism and image of the new army were seen very much as integral to the virtues of the new state. The National Army image improved and was noticed by the British military hierarchy and government who wished to help

---

[378]Dáil Éireann & Dáil Éireann Local Government files, NAI, D.E. 3/6/3 1919-30, accounts of the director of organisation 1921-25.

[379]Vincent MacDowell, *Michael Collins and the Irish Republican Brotherhood* (Dublin, 1997), pp. 69-74

[380]Emmet Dalton 1898-1978 in D.J. Hickey & J.F. Doherty, *A dictionary of Irish history 1800-1980* (Dublin, 1987), p.112

[381]Donal MacCarron, *Wings over Ireland: The story of the Irish Air Corps* (Leicester, 1996), pp. 6-27; Teddy Fennelly, *Fitz and the famous flight* (Portlaoise, 1997), pp. 19-118.

by influencing the way its officer corps was prepared for leadership. A colonial office dispatch dated 2 May 1923 offered a limited number of places to the Irish Free State government to send candidates to the Sandhurst Military Academy and the Royal Military College. It stated that,

'the Governor General of the other self governing dominions except the Irish Free State is empowered to recommend suitable candidates ... we enquire whether the Free State would desire same right'[382]

The Irish Governor General accepted the offer on 22 May 1923 with the criteria for recommendation requiring that the candidates must, among other things, be the sons of British subjects and be of pure European descent. They were to be sons of established and resident Irish Free State families and not of parents where 'connections with the dominion are only temporary or official'. Three candidates were to be accepted twice yearly to both colleges and later to the Royal Air Force College at Cramwell. The scheme was ended in June 1928 by the Free State with one of the reasons being that most candidates were below the standards required for nomination by the Irish Governor General. This shows a level of co-operation between the two governments and a desire by the Irish Army to acquire an education through the training of its officers in the British military schools. It was probably done so as to have influence later on and to negate the impact of IRA officers. One further interesting point on the topic of Irish soldiers and British service from this time can be found in the J. J. O'Connell papers in the National Library of Ireland. It is fact that the British Army regularly recruited in the South of Ireland during and after this period for its active service units to serve abroad but it may be that the Irish Guards Regiment were actively recruiting ex-National Army soldiers as late as 1931 and possibly later. This was the exact opposite to what was

---

[382]Governor Generals files, NAI, F.213, Colonial Office dispatch to Governor General 2 May 1923

happening in 1922-1923.[383] The army was seen as proficiently experienced enough to warrant a kind of headhunting by one of the most famous operational units of the British Army.

Mutiny

The genesis of the army mutiny of 1924 lay in the circumstances of its creation and hasty expansion in 1922-1923 to secure the territory of the state and fight the Civil War. Post conflict demobilisation also contributed. Winston Churchill, in the House of Commons, had earlier stated that 'under the treaty an army of between 30,000 and 40,000 men was not seen to have been in excess of the provision, which Ireland is entitled to make.' 'After some time, if special needs arose of a larger force to suppress the present condition of dissent in Ireland the government would feel perfectly at liberty to consider a larger force'.[384]

The estimated strength of the army in early 1922 was 25,000, with 2,286 in various stages of training.[385] By the final violent contortions of the Civil War the army strength stood at 55,000 men. The proposed demobilisation of the army from its final strength by over 20,000 soldiers to 31,000 in January 1924 began smoothly with the transition of NCOs and men to civilian life. But this changed when officers began to be let go. Three classes of officers were designated in descending order of dismissal (a) officers whose work was unsatisfactory, (b) post-Truce officers who had no special qualifications and (c) pre-Truce officers who were surplus to requirements. One of the results of the mass demob of officers was an internal dispute between old IRA veterans and the newly reconstituted

---

[383]J.J. O' Connell papers, NLI, Ms.22,148, letter from Col D. Neligan C.O.S. branch to Col S. O' Higgins A.G.'s reference alleged recruiting by Irish Guards of ex-national army men, dated 193

[384]See clause 8 of the Anglo-Irish Treaty, *The parliamentary debates* 23 March 1922, fifth series, *House of Commons,* 20 Mar. -7 Apr. 1922 (London, 1922), p. 643, *The parliamentary debates,* fifth series, *House of Commons,* 24 July- 4 Aug. 1922 (London, 1922), p.65a

[385]For cabinet reports on defence in 1922 see Mulcahy papers, UCDA, P7/B/258-259

IRB and their influence over the direction of the army. The IRA officers formed themselves into the Irish Republican Army Organisation (IRAO). They felt that Collins's 'stepping stone' theory was being discounted, that old IRA veterans were being unfairly treated by being dismissed or passed over for promotion, particularly by ex-British officers and that they themselves had no influence on military policy. Over sixty officers absconded from their posts, taking vast amounts of weaponry and other material with them. For instance, the following table will show the type of war making material taken from Baldonnel and Gormanston bases alone.

Material Taken from Baldonnell and Gormanston Military Bases Only During 1924 Army Crisis[386]

	Taken	Returned	Missing
Lewis Guns	4	3	1
Lewis Guns Magazines	46	46	0
Bayonets	21	21	0
Web Equipment	2 Sets	2 Sets	0
Ammo .303	7500	7500	0
Lewis Guns Spares	1 Bag	1 Bag	0
Rifles	27	27	0

Although it was not a mutiny in the strictest sense, it did however have repercussions. But one must realise that the army needed experienced men. It had just extracted itself from an independence struggle, reforming on the lines of a conventional force in conflict with a guerrilla force in the field. The army needed to draw on the experience of people who had the training to fight this kind of war. During discussions with other people who have an historical interest in the

---

[386]Department of *An Taoiseach* files, NAI, S.3678A, B, C, & D, Dail debates on Irish army mutiny 26 March 1924 and discussions on war making material taken from military locations during army crisis of 1924 and which were still unaccounted for at the time

period, I have come to the conclusion that the Free State Army in 1923 could have contained up to 50 percent ex-British soldiers, potentially up to 20,000 to 25,000 men. Some correspondence from Irish Military Archives on this topic does admit that there was the potential for this figure.[387] Although this figure cannot be found in any primary source or confirmed in any contemporary document one can justify it by realising the amount of ex-soldiers in Ireland and the desire to recruit as many of them as possible when the opportunity arose, by an eager and desperate government and as Jane Leonard writes

> *"the outbreak of the Civil War was a catalyst for rallying ex-servicemen behind the Irish Free State . . . Its officer corps between 1923 and 1924 included more than 600 veterans of the Great War. Most of these had been rankers or subalterns but commissions were willingly issued to five who had commanded brigades on the western front.*[388]

If nothing else, they brought an element of discipline and professionalism to the army, which did not always possess such necessary military facets during the war. At a higher level, the planning, training, logistics, officer-ship and general-ship of ex-British officers in the army would have brought a different leadership ethos. The IRA must have heeded the importance of ex-British officers to the army as during the conflict Liam Lynch, IRA Chief of Staff, issued orders for all ex-British officers to be shot on sight.[389]

---

[387]Copy of letter from Military Archives of Ireland to Margaret Stewart Galway dated 2000 and quoting same, a copy of this letter is with author

[388]Jane Leonard Survivors in *"Our war: Ireland and the Great War"* ed John Horne (RIA, Dublin 2008) pp211-223

[389]O'Malley papers, UCDA, p17a/22

The committee which was set up in response to the so-called army mutiny found that one of the mutineers' primary reasons for organising was that they saw their government and especially the army as being taken over by British spies and ex-British soldiers. Generals Tobin and Dalton the principal leaders of the mutiny had complained of this. They saw these ex-servicemen being given the best and most important jobs while people like themselves, who had been dedicated to the cause of Irish freedom and who had fought all the way through the Irish War of Independence and Civil War, were now being sidelined in preference for their old enemy.[390] They saw ex-British Soldiers being favourably treated and the 'toleration and encouragement of the IRB gave the mutineers an excuse to mutiny.'[391] The mass demobs and the effects this was having on the men and community was also worrying. An army report describes some of the prevailing feelings throughout the country

> *'The state of general poverty and distress still continue… in a southern town which provided over 200 recruits for the army in 1922 many of the ex-Irish National Army men (90%) have not had a days work since they were demobilised…They see those that they fought against living in comparative luxury on looted money. A big reaction against the government is the only result to be expected.'*[392]

This state of affairs combined with the potential fallout from an army mutiny and the disgruntled soldiers, who numbered thousands, had the government questioning the loyalty of the army and the media. The media postmortem of the mutiny portrayed some of the rhetoric.

---

[390]Cabinet inquiry into claims of demobilised officers, Mulcahy papers, NAI, P7/C/2, UCDA; CAB 2/22; Dept of *Taoiseach* papers, NAI, S. 3678E, Army mutiny records of commission of inquiry

[391]Ibid

[392]Intelligence and mutiny papers MAI, Box 1, Fortnightly summary no.18 period ending 10 Feb. 1924, Office of the director of intelligence GHQ to chief of staff 16 Dec. 1924

The Belfast Newsletter stated,

'...the army regards Michael Collins as its spiritual leader... they were alarmed at the way the national position had been allowed to drift. Ex-British soldiers had been placed in high positions while those who had made government possible were forced out or put in minor positions... the army council had done its best to provoke rash action... The plain truth is that for the safety and stability of the government and the maintenance of law and order in the Free State the gunman element of the army must now be got rid off. The Tobin's and Dalton's and all the others who boast that they won the "Anglo-Irish War" are wholly unfitted by what they did in that war and by their claims based on that service, to hold any position of authority whatsoever in a permanent military force. The sooner the Free State government purges the army of all such, the better for itself and the country.'[393]

In an intelligence report to the army Chief of Staff that refers to the Irish Republican Army Organisation dated 26 March 1924, Tom Barry is quoted in a speech on the IRAO as accusing the GOC Cork of favouring ex-British officers.[394] In response to these complaints the committee heard from a number of people who gave evidence to the enquiry and came to the conclusion that in fact, as they saw it, only a few ex-British officers had been retained after the Civil War.[395] They found that the dissidents had used this issue as propaganda to foment dissatisfaction and unite desperate individuals who were unhappy with the demobilisation of the post-war army.[396] Obviously officers would hold the most desirable jobs so at that level in the hierarchy there would be few positions. There would have been hundreds more

---

[393]*Belfast Newsletter,* 12 Mar. 1924; Dept of *Taoiseach* papers, NAI, S.3694

[394]Mutiny papers, MAI, Box 1, monthly intelligence reports of director of army intelligence to army C.O.S. dated 26 Mar. 1924 refers to IRAO in army 08 Dec 1925- 08 Jan 1926

[395]For an official report of parliamentary debates on facts of the mutiny see Mulcahy papers, UCDA, P7a/129

[396]Valiulis, p. 226.

positions for ex-servicemen to fill in the enlisted ranks. With the seriousness of the situation to the security of the state the press discussed the situation.

The Morning Post said,

> *'The answer is simple. The summoning of General O'Duffy is the constitutionalists last throw of the dice... we cannot trust the army... they say in effect our only hope is in the unarmed Civic Guard. O'Duffy knows nothing about war so the DMP will be asked to contribute General Murphy who knows quite a lot about war to the work of rescue. In this way the Imperial Commonwealth of Southern Ireland may be saved for a while.'*[397]

According to General Sean McMahon, a former Chief of Staff, the number of ex-officers from other armies who had been retained in the army was 155, of which 80 had pre-Truce service. Of the remaining 75 officers 40 were technical officers with specialised skills that the army needed, such as medical and legal training. Furthermore he estimated that before reorganisation the army had been composed of approximately 25 per cent post-Truce and 75 per cent pre-Truce officers. After reorganisation approximately 90 per cent were pre-Truce and only 10 per cent post-Truce.[398] There is no other real qualifying or contrary evidence for this, so these figures must remain questionable, but if one assumes that the number of enlisted or ordinary soldiers will always be much greater in number than that of the smaller nucleus of officers needed to lead, then one can see that a larger figure of ex-British soldiers with essential experience were involved in the army during the Civil War. If viewed in a manner of military reactionary thinking then one can see that the government

---

[397]*Morning Post*, 14 Mar. 1924

[398]Valiulis, p. 274; One can check statements of some individual officers in the Army Inquiry papers, UCDA, i.e. Officer Commanding Army Corps of Engineers P7/C/18; Lt Col Ryan commander training and operations P7/C/8

needed to build up the army's strength quickly to secure the country.[399] If 155 officers from foreign armies are quite sufficient to have a considerable impact, imagine the effect the true figure would have had.

The Civic Guard that replaced the DMP and RIC also had ex-soldiers as well as ex-RIC men and as a result the same feelings existed towards them. Of the almost 1,500 men who joined the Civic Guard in its own pre-mutiny period of February until the end of May 1922, 86.1 percent had an IRA background, 3 percent had been in the RIC, 3.6 per cent had RIC and IRA backgrounds, 0.4 per cent had British Amy service and 1 per cent had both British Amy and IRA service and many of those had transferred from the army.[400]

As with the army, recruitment policy for the police was the result of pragmatism. Although the Guards recruited specifically, as policy, from the IRA, it needed people with military experience who were used to a disciplined regime. The later constituted Garda (Civil Police) authorities welcomed ex-soldiers in the beginning but after 1934 this continued at a reduced rate. The National Army realised the same necessities but had a greater mass of people to recruit and train. As had happened with the Guards, when the disgruntlement within the army came to a head in 1924 because of the perceived mass retention and promotions of ex-soldiers, at the same time as the forced demobilisations, there was mutiny. On the mutiny the Sunday Observer noted,

'The army is lacking a tradition which is the most valuable part of military education…mutiny leaders did not know what they were doing. In the Irish Army very high commands are held by very young men, who have not much experience because the conditions of life in the country have not given a chance for civic qualities to develop such questions as the relationship of the army to the civic

---

[399]The Mulcahy papers, UCDA, P7/B/153, hold documents showing national army strength was estimated in Dec. 1922 at 72,000-80,000 and some claimed 100,000, General O' Duffy claimed a week before the treaty at 110,000; MP, UCDA, P7/B/189; Peter Long Thesis

[400]Liam McNiffe, *A history of the Garda Siochana*, (Dublin, 1997), pp 33-35

power have never been before us to consider. There is said to be the complaint of "Anglicising the army, but of this phenomenon the outside observer can detect little trace except the influence of British drill. All or practically all the important commands are held by men whose only service has been in Ireland against England." [401]

In a pamphlet published by the mutineers titled 'The Truth About the Army Crisis' they argued that the army was being built up of largely anti-national elements,[402] ceasing to be a National Army and being officered by and recruited from ex-British soldiers, some of whom they had fought against in the War of Independence.[403] They also saw active army men who had been active British secret service agents.[404] Many senior officers resigned in protest against demobilisation of the old IRA while ex-British soldiers were being retained.[405] There were even descriptions of 'the Irish loyalists of tomorrow in the Free State' circulated.[406]

The 'Tobinites' spread conspiracy theories that the IRB was reorganising and had taken control of the army and there were rumours of Masonic influences through ex-British officers protecting their own interests.[407] There were some members of Masonic orders in the Irish Army but like Francis Annessly, who had also served in the merchant

---

[401]*Sunday Observer,* 16 Mar. 1924

[402]Dept of *An Taoiseach,* NAI, S.3678A – D, Dail debates on army inquiry 1924

[403]Mulcahy papers, UCDA, P7/C/3, cabinet enquiry into claims of demobilised officers in regular army

[404]Dept of *An Taoiseach,* NAI, S.3678A –D, Dail debates on army inquiry 1924

[405]Mulcahy papers, UCDA, P7/C/8,L Letters of resignation to president in protest at demobilisation of old IRA while ex- British being retained

[406]Mulcahy papers, UCDA, P7/B/344 'At the time of the boundary agreement a special unit formed in the Curragh under the command of an officer, who had served in the British Army. Its men were all quite of a different stamp from those who had a more nationalist outlook. Known as the "Border Unit" it lasted for about a year';
The Sunday Press, 31 Oct. 1965

[407]Mulcahy papers, UCDA, P7/B/140, director of intelligence report on OIRA, 6 Nov. 1923; O' Halpin, p.47.

navy, they did not necessarily have previous military service.[408] The IRB was being reformed, but this was being done so as to save it from being used by others. Mulcahy saw it as a way of preventing it falling into the wrong hands. A secret organisation was the last thing the army needed within its ranks. Just before the mutiny one disgruntled officer was quoted as saying in reference to former British and post-Truce officers in positions of authority, 'Every fighting man in Dublin is leaving the army if those snobs are kept on.'[409]

However, these senior officers saw much of their discontent through blinkered eyes and attributed some of the blame to ex-British servicemen. But these ex-servicemen had helped shorten the war and brought about a semi-stable environment. There has always been a large element of Anglophobia in Ireland. The anti-Treaty side felt no different at the time; in fact there was a heightened sense of it. England, in their opinion was a decadent society and was also the natural enemy. There was a long tradition of fighting between the Gael and the Gall. The army of 1913 and 1921 was a symbol of the neo-Gaelic society that the republicans wished to identify with and illuminate. The Irish Army was seen as being very Irish or of the Irish-Ireland theme and part of the ideology of the Gaelicised Irish civilisation.

However, post 1922 the Irish Army was made up of ex-British servicemen. Those Anglicised and tainted soldiers certainly did not fit into this ideology and were seen as part of the Anglo-Irish ascendancy plot beginning all over again. But Sinn Féin, the Gaelic League and republicans knew very little about Ireland's Gaelic past. The history of Ireland that people were aware of at the turn of the 20th century is very different to what is taught today. It is only because of the research and scholarship of the 20th century that we have any clear understanding

[408]Francis J. Annessly, NLI, MS-21, 935, Masonic Order in Dublin, courier in merchant navy and officer in Irish Army

[409]Michael Hopkinson, *Green against green,* p. 226

of Gaelic culture and society and they are not in keeping with ideologies of any kind.[410] This has been another reason for the impact of ex-British soldiers being written out of Irish historiography. After his death at mBéal na Bláth, Collins's funeral in Glasnevin on 28 August 1922 attracted huge crowds, but his official reputation until quite recently was a miserable one. De Valera did what he could to play down Collins's impact, reputation and significance while he was in power. Successive governments did everything they could to hinder the Collins family from erecting a suitable memorial over his grave, a simple military grave.

Ann Dolan has established in her excellent book *'Commemorating the Irish Civil War; History and Memory, 1923-2000'* how the memory of Free State soldiers of the National Army who died during the conflict had been neglected, as opposed to the way the Republican sacrifice was remembered. Collins's grave was for a long time the only one to be remembered and only after a very long struggle, but the Republican sacrifice had always been acknowledged.[411] If the national troops were not commemorated then what chance had the soldier who served in the army who had British training and experience? As late as the mid 1960s publications by the Department of Foreign Affairs, like the handbook 'Facts about Ireland', had no photograph of Collins. He had been cast into the wilderness so to speak but this has changed as a result of the Neil Jordan movie depicting Collins's career.[412] Collins is once again a national icon but there is not much detail on the National Army and nothing on the British army veteran's service in the Irish Army after 1913.

---

[410]Garvin, *Nationalist revolutionaries in Ireland,* pp110-111

[411]Anne Dolan, *Commemorating the Irish Civil War: history and memory, 1923-2000* (New York, 2003)

[412]Purdon, pp 44-5, The Michael Collins movie directed by Neil Jordan was released in 1996.

Henry Stewart's discharge papers. *Courtesy of Margaret Stewart.*

William O'Reilly (left) Punjab, *(right)* William O'Reilly prisoner of War.
Courtesy of Eilish Lambe.

Commissioner O'Duffy & Senior Officers, taken in 1925.

Front left to right: Assistant Commissioner P Walsh, Commissioner E. O'Duffy, Deputy Commissioner E. Coogan
Back: Assistant Commissioner E Cullen, Deputy Commissioner W.R.E. Murphy

Courtesy of the Garda Press Office.

Jim Fitzgerald in British Army uniform during WWI.
Courtesy of Jimmy Hayles.

Captain James Fitzmaurice.
Courtesy of the Irish Air Corps.

Pilot at Baldonnel. *Courtesy of the Irish Air Corps.*

Airmen at Baldonnel. *Courtesy of the Irish Air Corps.*
Left to right: Tosty Gogan, Jackie Hume, Oscar Heron (ex-RAF), Ned Stapleton, Billy Delamere (ex-RAF), James Fitzmaurice (ex-RAF), Dan McKeown, Ned Fogarty, Ted Crossley (ex-RAF), Dr. Theo McWeeney, Serg Barnes, Arthur Russell, Gerry Carroll (ex-RAF), Brian McSweeney, Frank McGrath, Tim Prenderville.

The Freeman's Journal

ESTD. 1763.] IRELANDS NATIONAL NEWSPAPER [ESTD. 1763

DUBLIN: TUESDAY, AUGUST 1, 1922.

OGLAIGH na h-EIREANN.
VOLUNTEER RESERVE.

VOLUNTARY LEVY, JULY, 1922.

PUBLIC NOTICE.

In order to complete the quota for the undermentioned Brigade, Recruiting for the Volunteer Reserve has been resumed at the following addresses:—

No. 3 CHARLEMONT TERRACE, DUN LAOGHAIRE
TALLAGHT (Aerodrome) CAMP, TALLAGHT
GREYSTONES COASTGUARD STATION
CHURCH STREET BARRACKS, WICKLOW
AVONDALE HOUSE, RATHDRUM
ARKLOW COASTGUARD STATION

As only a limited number of recruits are required to complete the quota, those desirous of joining should report at once at one of the above Recruiting Stations.

TERMS OF SERVICE.

Pay—Two Shillings and Sixpence per day and all found. Dependent's allowance to married men in accordance with the circumstances of each case.

Recruits will proceed immediately after enrolment to a Training and Equipping Depot, where they will receive Uniform, Equipment, Rifle and Ammunition, and undergo a short course of training. They will then be available for active service in the Brigade Area or elsewhere for a PERIOD OF SIX MONTHS, after which they will return to their homes and civilian occupations. Having so returned, they will be liable to weekly parades (in the same way as hitherto with Volunteer Companies), and will form a Reserve, to be called up for active service in case of National Emergency.

Signed,—NIALL MacNEILL, Brigadier,
Commanding No. 2 Brigade, 2nd Eastern Division.

Harbour Barracks, Dun Laoghaire, Co. Dublin.

Captain James Fitzmaurice and the Bremen crew with Kaiser.
Courtesy of the Irish Air Corps.

The Bremen. *Courtesy of the Irish Air Corps.*

156

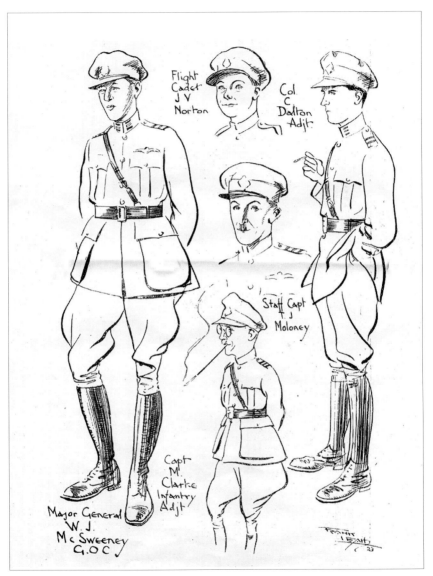

Caricatures of ex-British officers and the Republican Col. C. Dalton of the Irish Air Service. *An tÓglach 1923. Courtesy of Irish Military Archives.*

> **'It may not in fact be so surprising if, on examination, an Irish military tradition turns out to be central to the Irish historical experience, and a key element in modern Irish identity'**
>
> T. Bartlett & K. Jeffery, 'An Irish Military Tradition' in *A Military History of Ireland* (Cambridge, 1996), p.2

Chapter V

'because of his appointment as Commander in Chief of the Irish Army, the work carried out by others was always overshadowed. It was not always politically possible to advertise the presence of those who had Foreign Service and as a result the contributions of such officers as Emmet Dalton and others have been neglected.'

Commandant Peter Young, Irish Military Archives, analysis of Michael Collins as a military leader[413]

O N the fiftieth anniversary of the 1916 Rising in 1966, Sean Lemass, the Taoiseach, who had fought in the Rising, in a speech he delivered in Dublin in the presence of President Eamon de Valera, the British Ambassador and the US Ambassador, spoke to his audience of the 'generous young Irishmen who had volunteered enthusiastically to fight, as they believed, for the Liberty of Belgium'. He added,

'In later years it was common – and I also was guilty in this respect – to question the motives of those men who joined the new British armies formed at the outbreak of the war, but it must, in their honour, and in fairness to their memories, be said that they were motivated by the highest purpose, and died in their tens of thousands in Flanders and Gallipoli, believing they were giving their lives in the cause of human liberty everywhere, not excluding Ireland'[414]

---

[413]Comdt Peter Young, *An Cosantóir review* Vol. 4 1997, p.141
[414]Henry Harris, Irish regiments, pp 211-212; Irish Times, April. 1966; Desmond and Jean Bowen, heroic option: the Irish in the British army, p.28

This book has highlighted the employment of ex-British servicemen in the Irish Army throughout its evolution. This service was one of the major factors that helped the IRA during the Irish War of Independence, thus helping to persuade the British government to negotiate. This is also true for the National Army during the Civil War. The terrible pain of a Civil War fought between old comrades will be palpable in any country but in a small state like Ireland it was very evident. Collins, as the leader of the National Army, and even the government were anxious to 'end the killing' and used all the resources at their disposal to stop the conflict.

Irish veterans of the British Army did not exactly fit into that old comrade fold. It should be remembered that they played a pivotal role during those volatile years at the inception of the Irish State and that all the way through the struggle for independence they were Irishmen; many of them nationalists and many had originally been members of the Volunteers in 1913. They went to fight for Britain on the promise of Home Rule for Ireland. When they returned some felt like outcasts, but found themselves fighting and in many cases actually leading the Irish army. They also trained the force throughout the period as it had evolved into the IRA and National Army. The IRA was a guerrilla force combating a conventional army by using British military skills learned from ex-British soldiers. The Irish army (National Army) fought the IRA, which it had also evolved from, representing a conventional military force using many more ex-British soldiers. They also utilised lessons they had learned from the War of Independence against the British. During the Civil War Republicans were fighting the very men who they had earlier fought side by side with and who knew their strategies and tactics and leaders.

The ex-British soldiers helped to transform the army from a guerrilla force into a conventional army. The ex-soldier brought a disciplined edge to the new army as well as the skills to use all the new material and weapons that the British government had provided. They even showed the soldiers how to wear the new state's national symbol for the army, its uniform. Those with the purely guerrilla background and who joined the National Army would not have known how to properly wear and maintain a uniform as per military regulations and etiquette. This is borne out in the many photographs of the period where both British and Irish soldiers were pictured together.

It is further illuminated through the study of just one iconic image of the time, the image of Michael Collins on the day of his appointment as Commander-in-Chief of the army as captured on film in Cathal Brugha Barracks in 1922 where the photograph shows him wearing the general's uniform for the first time. What is very interesting about this image is that the usually impeccably well groomed Collins, who was always conscious of the camera and who in most cases would pose for the shot, was on this most important of all days, quite the reverse. Collins was not familiar with wearing a uniform and as Comdt Peter Young also observed

'he is wearing a uniform that is missing a button and slacks that were too short. As it is well worn, I assume that it was borrowed, as any other photograph shows him in a well-fitted uniform. It just goes to underline the speed with which events were developing'.[415]

Collins does indeed look uncomfortable in the uniform and it seems like a hasty fit for the purpose of the photograph. If it was borrowed from one of the close entourage it may have come from Emmet Dalton or someone else in that group but needless to say those with British experience would most likely have had a more respectable and well-kept attire. The fact that Collins' presentation in later photographs shows a more prepared and tailored uniform may be as a result of careful consultation with and influence of his more militarily experienced officers. This professional image was needed and geared towards galvanising the army and portraying a symbol of leadership to the country and the outside world. An interesting aside to this is the theory that a number of senior British officers with the appropriate backgrounds were said to have been approached by Michael Collins with a view to becoming Commander-In-Chief of the new army. One of those is thought to have been the Irish lieutenant Colonel Henry Francis Jourdain, Commander of the Connaught Rangers at Renmore barracks, Galway and later of both the Boer War and Great War. This is interesting as one can imagine the outcome if indeed Jourdain or someone of those credentials had been appointed, this theory being correct of course. The anti-Treaty-ites and later the mutineers would have had a field day admonishing these English officers.

The army recruited many ex-servicemen during the war as policy. After the Treaty and the disbandment of Irish regiments in the British Army they had a pool of manpower to choose from. They managed to get the services of many senior officers including those of Generals W.R.E. Murphy, Emmet Dalton and others to lead the army, although Dalton had already been a member of the IRA in the conflict with the British. Senior members of the Free State government directly approached others. Eamon Coogan from Kilkenny, a Trinity College graduate who was working in the Department of Local Government was asked, by W.T. Cosgrave, to join the Guards in 1922 and was appointed Assistant Commissioner almost immediately. Coogan had already had a distinguished career in the British Army during World War I and had joined the National Army in 1922.[416] So also had a British officer named Pritchard who was alleged to have remained on in Ireland to help Michael Collins as an advisor and intelligence specialist, at his request, after the Treaty.[417]

During the Civil War, republican rhetoric, which had been used against the ex-servicemen in previous years, was intensified. The victimisation that had been a large part of the mistrust during the War of

[416]MacNiffe, pp 78-79
[417]O'Farrell, p.189

Independence carried on throughout the Civil War and beyond. Ex-British soldiers were fighting and dying in the army as Irishmen defending the Free State against an enemy. They were patriots also, but animosity towards ex-British soldiers serving in the army was not helped by the death of Michael Collins, under suspicious circumstances, in August 1922. General Emmet Dalton has since been compared to a double agent working for the British because of his previous history. John McPeak, another ex-British soldier involved in the defence of the ambush at mBéal na Bláth was also implicated.[418]

Conspiracy theories have been rife over the years that both these men were instrumental in Collins' death.[419] These theories have no basis and have never been proven. But behind the trend of victimisation and violence towards ex-servicemen there was a genuine need for their experience and skills from 1913 to the end of the Civil War in 1923. Their impact on the Irish Army can be simply explained as having been essential for the conduct of a rebellion, a War of Independence and a Civil War and in the latter case the defeat of anti-Treaty forces in the field.

However, their legacy has all but been forgotten. Their stories were never recorded in any other fashion. The Bureau of Military History contains over 1,700 witness statements of people who participated or otherwise witnessed events during 1913-1921. There was no such effort on anyone's behalf to take statements or record the stories of those who participated in the Irish Civil War; hence there is no real collection of material. As such the impact of the ex-British soldier on the Irish Civil War and army has been written out of Irish

---

[418]The area in Cork where the ambush of Collins' convoy occurred in August 1922

[419]Dept of *An Taoiseach* papers, NAI, S.3248, 9-25 Aug. 1923 McPeak was an ex-British serviceman and was implicated in Collins' death and arrested in Scotland on an Irish warrant; For example see John M. Feehan, *The shooting of Michael Collins, murder or accident* (Cork, 1981), pp 76-124; Vincent McDowell, *Michael Collins and the Irish republican brotherhood* (Dublin, 1997), pp133-52.

historiography of the period. No effort has been made since to rectify this nor has there been any real effort to record the story of the National Army in general.

In the 1920s and '30s many Irish men and women were struggling to cope with personal losses inflicted by ten years of war. During those years the new nation celebrated the achievements of 1916 and independence fighters. In contrast, Irishmen who had served in the Great War with the British Army attempted to conceal their military history. Those that later served in the new army during the Civil War could not hope to have their role recognised positively. The Treaty and Civil War politics had not only affected the ideologies and sense of identity of the army but also its sense of mission. The Treaty drew new lines of division across the hearts and minds of old comrades especially because of the intense form of violence involved. These divisions lasted for generations. The inclusion of veterans was more or less the key to the military victories and success on the ground; it was not just down to superior numbers, which the Free State possessed. And much of the rhetoric aimed at the government was directed towards ex-servicemen and what they were perceived to represent. As Tom Garvin put it,

> *'The fact that the Treaty was an extraordinary concession was scarcely understood by some IRA soldiers and radical ideologues, galvanised as they were by the expectations raised by the emotional rhetoric of the time. The fact that it marked the final defeat of Anglo- Ireland was also not fully grasped, partly because some among the nationalists could perhaps be seen as trying to step into the shoes of the ascendancy. Collins's desperate plea that the Treaty offered the "freedom to achieve freedom" was not always believed, and was sometimes denounced as a device to camouflage a continuation of Ascendancy Ireland under green symbols.'*[420]

---

[420]Tom Garvin, The aftermath of the Civil War: the Civil War 1922-23, in *The Irish Sword, the journal of the military history society of Ireland*, Vol. XX, no. 82 (Dublin, 1997), p.337

Garvin also sums up exactly the military strengths of the opposing anti-Treaty Irish army and the pro-Treaty Irish army after the IRA split,

> '*In part, the anti-Treaty IRA had local roots in a tradition of local solidarity much as had the pre-Treaty IRA. However, during the Civil War both sides had local contacts; the rather bewildered British, with their massive armaments, were replaced, from the IRA point of view, by men with local knowledge and almost equally impressive armaments.*
>
> *Local men faced local men, often wearing similar uniforms and often having bonds of affection. On the Free State side, however, was an army drawn from ex-British veterans, IRA veterans and the apolitical youth of the towns. The old cunning of the IRA leaders was in vain against the Free State's combination of similar cunning, weight of armaments and men.*'[421]

We can sum up some of the feelings towards those ex-British servicemen who served in the Free State army by looking at how the post war years and the memories of the Civil War affected the career of General W.R.E. Murphy. When he was appointed Commissioner of the Dublin Metropolitan Police in April 1923 it was despite major opposition from the old IRA list of 'objectionables'.[422] He later hoped that he would get the top job in the Garda Síochána also but the politics of the time was against him. His service was always appreciated but his past record in the National Army during the Civil War and his service in the British Army may have been too sensitive.[423]

---

[421]Ibid, p.389

[422]Taoiseach's Department papers, NAI, S9050

[423]Karl Murphy, (M.A. thesis), p.64; Major General W.R.E. Murphy, 'the local security force: its original purpose', in the call to arms: a historical record of Irelands defence services (Dublin, 1945), pp 187-191.

Tom Garvin elaborates,

> *'All the top posts in the new peace time army went to trusted personnel or to technical experts; British Army experts were quickly sidelined once their jobs were done. WRE Murphy, for example, the pacifier of Kerry, was given a senior post in the DMP and virtually written out of history, presumably to his own satisfaction'* [424]

Irishmen who survived the slaughter of the Great War came home to an Ireland that was utterly changed; a "terrible beauty" had been born in their absence. Attitudes to some of these men were at the least indifferent and at most, downright hostile, to a point where some were murdered. It is a fact that the majority of these men had seen enough bloodshed, sorrow and carnage in one lifetime, and they did not want to get caught up with more. They returned home to the empty promises of a decent place to live, a better life and a job.

Some of those who died in the war were lucky to have a grave. Many were never recovered, their remains were to become part of the sand in Gallipoli or the mud of Flanders, to be written out of Irish history and forgotten. Irish soldiers are buried in cemeteries large and small spread throughout the combat theatres of the world where they fell. In these cemeteries, maintained by the British Commonwealth War Graves Commission, there are visitor books for one to sign. Only recently and after a passage of almost nine decades can there be found in these books the names of visitors from Dublin, Cork or other places in the Republic of Ireland. Does this reflect an indifference to these men? Were they not Irishmen and patriots fighting for Ireland? They were but the goal posts had moved and they became outcasts.

Then there are those like Tom Barry who survived the Great War only to return as outcasts initially and do equally great things for Ireland at home and who have become national heroes. They are remembered

---

[424]Tom Garvin, 1922: the birth of Irish democracy, p.129

because of their republican credentials, which brought them back into the patriotic fold. Through their military guile and skills they found themselves among the most illustrious of those of Ireland's heroes with historical, mythical and legendary status. But what of men such as W.R.E. Murphy, MM, DSO, and Martin Doyle V.C. who were heroes and did great things for Ireland also. They are buried under British military headstones or gravestones commemorating their Great War service with no mention of their impact on the times they lived through in Ireland. Emmet Dalton is buried near Michael Collins but with the simple inscription of his name, nothing else, and nothing to say he was a soldier of Ireland. They have been forgotten by their countrymen and remembered only by their families, who never forget and former comrades of their previous service, who were also often to become their enemies.

If Ireland can finally remember Irish soldiers of foreign wars can we not now also honour the Irishmen from the British Army who, throughout the world, and later in Ireland fought for its many shades of honour and freedom during the period of independence? The adoption of the green white and orange flag as the national emblem of the Irish State, to this day symbolises the commitment of generations of Irish people who struggled for independence and the promise of freedom in its many capacities and forms, not least those in the period 1913-1924.[425]

The Irish Defence Force of today owes its origins to the volunteers of 1913, 1914, 1916 and 1922. It owes its conventional and professional ethos to the ex-servicemen of the British Army of that same period. The modern Irish Army can be described as a small, guerrilla type, conventionally trained force, incorporating both styles of military doctrine in its training. It has much to be grateful for but much baggage to carry also. The commissioning of officers in Britain is by the Queen as head of state and therefore based on a feudal style, making the

[425]Dept. of *An Taoiseach* Papers, NAI, S3088A, adoption of national flag, 9 Jan, 1923 - 18 Oct, 1934.

officer corps a class apart as leaders. All those in the military and nation are British subjects. In Ireland the commissioning of officers to the national forces is by the president as head of state of a republic, elected by the people and therefore for the people. Like the British and Americans on commissioning he is an officer and a gentleman but at the same time, he is equal to every other citizen within the Irish State, as the sovereign is the Irish people. They are commissioned as leaders and managers for the protection of the integrity of the Irish people and by extension the state and no class distinction should come to bear except the respect for military rank. This is a direct legacy of the period but there is a thread of class difference. The army today could so easily have been like the traditional British model but it chose to have the professionalism and nationalism without too much of a transparent ascendancy although threads of this still exist. Although Ireland became a republic in 1949 the army has in some cases failed to reflect this and still contains some threads of the old style conventions brought in by ex-British officers and NCOs in the 1920s.

Unlike the Americans, the Irish Defence Forces, enshrined in the constitution as the only legal and legitimate military force in the Republic of Ireland does not yet contain the apparatus allowing soldiers of lower enlisted rank to achieve positions in the highest offices of commissioned power. It is quite difficult for an enlisted man or woman to attain commissioned rank, even after many years of service, no matter what the experience or educational background and in effect it comes down to pedigree and not what a soldier can provide to enhance the military.

However, the army has always been enfeebled by the Civil War and its politics. Like the ex-British servicemen in this study, the Irish Army was not trusted. They had the greatest impact on the Volunteers and IRA in militarising the movement and in bringing the British to the negotiating table. Ex-British were also responsible for the disciplining of the Irish Army and in doing so helped it to become subservient to the civil authorities after the Irish Civil War. Their loyalties and allegiances were always compromised, even when serving in the British Army, because after 1916 Irish soldiers were no longer trusted as they once were. This British service was to be held against them always, especially within the evolutionary Irish Army.

Grave of Emmet Dalton, WWI veteran, ex-IRA and National Army.
Photo Kieran Swords.

Bibliography

Primary Sources

Military Archives of Ireland
Army Census 1922
Army Mutiny Papers 1924
Bureau of Military History 1913-1921
Michael Collins Papers

National Archives of Britain
Colonial Office papers CO 904, British in Ireland series (Held on microfilm in NUI Maynooth)

National Archives of Ireland
Bureau of Military History 1913-1921
Dáil Éireann & Dáil Éireann Local Government Papers
Department of Taoiseach Papers

National Library of Ireland Manuscript Room
Bulmer Hobson Papers
Erskine Childers Papers
Florence O' Donoghue Papers
Michael Collins Papers
Piaras Beaslaí Papers

Trinity College Dublin Manuscript Room
Dublin University Officer Training Corps Papers 1912-1922
Erskine Childers Papers
Patrick Pearse Papers

University College Dublin
Dan Bryan papers
Eamon de Valera Papers
Ernie O' Malley Papers
Fitzgerald papers
Frank Aiken Papers
Richard Mulcahy papers
Sean McEoin Papers

NEWSPAPERS

Belfast Newsletter
Daily Mail
Daily Press
Free Man's Journal
Irish Independent
Irish Times
Morning Post
Poblacht Na hEireann, War News
Sunday Observer
The Free Press
The Sunday Press
Wexford People

GOVERNMENT

Irish Government stationary office, *Bunreacht Na hÉireann* – Constitution of Ireland (Dublin, 1999)

The Parliamentary Debates, fifth series, *House of Commons,* 10 April-May12 1922, (vol. 153) (London, 1922)

The parliamentary debates, fifth series, *House of Commons,* 20 November- 25 December 1922 (vol.159), (London, 1923)

Papers of the British Parliamentary Archive, 'the Irish Uprising 1914-21'in *Uncovered Editions* (London Stationary Office, 2000)

Secondary Sources

PUBLISHED MATERIAL

Augusteijn, Joost, *From Public defiance to guerrilla warfare: t*he *experience of ordinary volunteers in the Irish War of Independence* 1916-1921 (Dublin, 1996)

Augusteijn, Joost, Ed., *The Irish Revolution 1913-23* (London, 2002)

Beever, Antony, *The Spanish Civil War* (2nd ed., London, 1999)

Bennett, Douglas, *Encyclopaedia of Dublin* (Dublin, 1991)

Bennett, Richard, *The Black and Tans* (Kent, 2001)

Bowen, Desmond and Jean, *Heroic option: the Irish in the British Army* (Yorkshire, 2005)

Brown, Terence, Ireland: *A Social and Cultural History 1922-2002* (London, 2004)

Carey, Tim, *Hanged for Ireland: the forgotten ten, executed 1920-21,* a documentary history (Dublin, 2001)

Childers, Erskine, *Military Rule in Ireland* (Dublin, 1920)

Coogan, Tim Pat, *An officers wife in Ireland* (Dublin, 1984)

Coogan, Tim Pat and Morrison, George, *The Irish Civil War* (2nd ed., London, 1999)
Coogan, Tim Pat, *1916: Easter Rising* (London, 2005)

Comerford, Richard, Vincent, *Ireland* (London, 2003)

Connolly, Colm, *Michael Collins* (Great Britain 1996)

Costello, Con, *A most delightful station: the British Army on the Curragh of Kildare, Ireland 1855-1922* (Cork, 1996)

Cottrell, Peter, 'The Anglo-Irish War, the troubles of 1913-1922' in *Osprey essential histories series* (Oxford, 2006), p.85

Cronin, Sean, *Kevin Barry,* (2nd ed., Dublin, 2001)

Davies, Norma, *Europe a history* (Oxford, 1997)

deBurca, Padraig and Boyle, John, F., *Free State or Republic* (Dublin, 2002)

de Rosa, Peter, Rebels: *The Irish Rising of 1916* (Dublin, 2000)

Doherty, Richard, *IRA volunteers in the Second World War* (Australia, 2002)

Doyle, David, Noel, and Edwards, Owen, Dudley, (eds.), *America and Ireland 1776-1976: The American identity and the Irish connection: the proceedings of the United States bicentennial conference of Cumann Merriman,* Ennis August 1976 (Connecticut, 1980)

Duffy, Sean, (ed.), *Atlas of Irish history* (2nd ed., Dublin, 2000)

Duggan, John P., *A history of the Irish Army* (Dublin, 1991)

Durney, James, *On the one road: political unrest in Kildare 1913-1996* (Naas, 2001)

Dwyer, T. Ryle, *The squad and the intelligence operations of Michael Collins* (Cork, 2005)

Ellis, Peter, Beresford, *Eyewitness to Irish history* (New Jersey, 2004)

Evans, Martin, Marix, *The military heritage of Britain and Ireland* (2nd ed., Great Britain, 2004)

Evans, Martin, Marix, *A terrible beauty: an iIllustrated history of Irish battles* (Dublin, 2003)

Evans, Martin, Marix, *Passchaendale and the Battles of Ypres 1914 –18* (London, 1997)

Feehan, John, M., *The shooting of Michael Collins, murder or accident* (Cork, 1981)

Foster, R.F., *Modern Ireland: 1600- 1972* (London, 1988)

Foster, R.F., *The Oxford history of Ireland* (Oxford, 1989)

Garvin, Tom, *The evolution of Irish Nationalist politics* (2nd ed., Dublin, 2005)

Garvin, Tom, *Nationalist revolutionaries in Ireland 1858-1978* (2nd ed., Oxford, 2005)

Garvin, Tom, 1922: *The birth of Irish democracy* (2nd ed., Dublin, 2005)

George, David Lloyd, *War memoirs of David Lloyd George* (vol. II, Great Britain, n.d.)

Gialanella, Valiulis, Maryann, *General Richard Mulcahy: portrait of a revolutionary* (Dublin, 1992), p. 182

Girvin, Brian and Roberts, Geffrey (eds.), *Ireland and the Second World War: politics, society and remembrance* (Dublin, 2000)

Hanley, Brian, *A guide to military heritage: Maynooth research guides for Irish local history* (Dublin, 2004)

Hart, Peter, *The IRA and its enemies: violence and community in Cork 1916-1923* (USA, 1998)

Hart, Peter, *The IRA at War 1916-1923* (USA, 2003)

Haughton, John, *The silver lining, Lady Heath: Kildonan-a golden age of flying* (Ireland, 2003)

Helferty, Seamus and Gillespie, Raymond (eds.) *Directory of Irish archives (3rd ed.,* Ireland, 1993)

Henig, Ruth, 'The origins of the First World War', in *Lancaster Pamphlets* (3rd ed., London, 2002)

Henry, William, *Supreme sacrifice: the story of Eamon Ceannt 1881-1916* (Cork, 2005)

Hobsbawm, Eric, *The age of empire 1875-1914* (3rd ed., Great Britain, 1994)

Hobsbawm, Eric, *Age of extremes the short twentieth century 1914- 1991* (2nd ed., Great Britain, 1995)

Hogan, James, J., *Badges, medals, insignia of the Irish Defence Forces* (Dublin, 1987)

Holmes, Richard (ed.) *The Oxford companion to military history* (USA, 2001)

Hopkinson, Michael, *Green against green, The Irish Civil War* (2nd ed., Dublin, 1988)

Hopkinson, Michael, *The Irish War of Independence,* 2nd ed. (Dublin, 2004)

I.O., *The administration in Ireland* (London, 1921)

Irish Air Corps, *The Irish Air Corps celebrates 100 Years* (Air Corps, 2003)

Jordan, Anthony, I., *Boer War to Easter Rising: the writings of John MacBride* (Westport, 2006)

Joy, Sinead, *The IRA in Kerry 1916-1821* (Cork, 2005)

Kenny, Kevin, Ed. *Ireland and the British Empire, Oxford History of the British Empire Companion Series* (Oxford, 2004)

Kostik, Conor and Collins, Lorcan, *The Easter Rising: a guide to Dublin in 1916* (Dublin, 2000)

Leonard, Jane 'Facing the finger of scorn: veterans memories of Ireland after the Great War, in Martin Evans and Ken Lunn (eds.) *War and memory in the twentieth century* (Oxford, 1997), pp 59-73;

Lyons, F.S.L., *Ireland since the Famine* (London, 1985)

Mansergh, Martin, *The legacy of history* (Cork, 2003)

Martin, Ira, *Political geography* (USA, 1993)

McArdle, Dorothy, *The Irish Republic* (6th ed., Dublin, 1999)

MacCarron, Donal, *A view from above: 200 years of aviation in Ireland* (Dublin, 2000)

MacCarron, Donal, *The Irish Defence Forces Since 1922* (Great Britain, 2004)

Martin, F. X., and Byrne, F. J., Eds. *The scholarly revolutionary Eoin McNeill 1867-1945 and the making of the New Ireland* (Dublin, 1973)

McDowell, Vincent, *Michael Collins and the Irish Republican Brotherhood* (Dublin, 1997)

McGarry, Fearghal, *Eoin O'Duffy: a self made hero* (Oxford, 2005)

Moody, T. W. and Martin, F.X., *The course of Irish history* (Dublin, 2001)

Moore, Stephen, *The Irish on the Somme, a battlefield guide to the Irish Regiments in the Great War and monuments to their memory* (Belfast, 2005)

Morrisson, George, *The Irish Civil War: an illustrated history* (2nd ed., Dublin, 1982)

Mulcahy, Risteard, *Richard Mulcahy, a family memoir* (Dublin, 1995)

Murphy, John A., *Ireland in the twentieth century* (Dublin, 1985)

Laffen Michael, *The resurrection of Ireland, The Sinn Fein Party 1916-1923* (New York, 2005)

Neeson, Eoin, *Birth of a Republic* (Dublin, 1998)

Nelson, John, *Michael Collins the final days* (Dublin, 1997)

O' Connor, John, *The 1916 Proclamation* (2nd ed., Dublin, 1999)

O'Connor, Ulick, *Oliver ST John Gogarty* (3rd ed. London, 1965)

O'Donoghue, Florence, *No other law* (Dublin, 1954)

O' Farrell, Mick, *A walk through rebel Dublin 1916* (Dublin, 1999)

O'Farrell, Padraig, *Who's who in the Irish War of Independence and Civil War 1916-1923 (Dublin, 1997)*

O' Gadhra, Nollaig, *Civil War in Connacht 1922-1923* (Cork, 1999)

O'Halpin, Eunan, *Defending Ireland: The Irish State and its enemies since 1922* (USA, 1999)

Pakenham, Thomas, *The Boer War* (4th ed., Great Britain, 1992)

Pope, Stephen and Wheal, Elizabeth–Anne, *The Macmillan Dictionary of the First World War* (London, 1997)

Robertshaw, Andrew, *A soldiers life through the ages: a visual history of soldiers through the ages* (Great Britain, 1997)

Ryan, Annie, *Witness: inside the Easter Rising* (Dublin, 2005)

Ryan, Desmond, *Sean Treacy and the 3rd Tipperary Brigade* (Tipperary, ?)

Ryan, Meda, *The day Michael Collins was shot* (Dublin, 2005)

Share, Bernard, *The emergency, neutral Ireland 1939-45* (Dublin, 1978)

Strachen, Hew, *The First World War* (Great Britain, 2003)

Taber, Robert, *The War of the flea: guerrilla warfare theory and practice* (Great Britain, 1970)

Tayler, James W., *The 1st Royal Irish Rifles in the Great War* (Dublin, 2002)

Tormey, Peter, Commandant, and Byrne, Kevin, Captain, *The Irish Air Corps: A view from the tower* (Dublin, 1991)

Townsend, Charles, *The British Campaign in Ireland 1919-21: The development of political and military policies in Oxford Historical Monographs* (London, 1975)

White, G., and O' Shea, B., 'The Irish Volunteer Soldier 1913 –23,' in *Osprey Warrior Series* (Great Britain, 2003)

Willmott, H.P., *First World War* (Great Britain, 2003)

Wood, Ian, S., *Ireland during the Second World War* (London, 2002)

Articles in Journals

Byrne, Liam, Cpl, 'An Irish soldier remembered, in *An Cosantóir: The Defence Forces Magazine,* Special 1916 Edition (Dublin, 1991), pp 28-31

Farrell, Theo, 'The model army: military imitation and the enfeeblement of the army in post- revolutionary Ireland 1922-42, in *Irish studies in international affairs,* vol. viii, (1997), pp 111-128

Murphy, Karl, 'An Irish General: William Richard English Murphy, 1890-1975', in *History Ireland,* vol. xiii no.3 (Dublin 2005), pp 10-11

O' Brien, Barry, Captain, 'The origins and development of the Cadet School 1929-1979, in A Special Edition of the *An Cosantóir, The Irish Defence Journal,* vol. xxxix no. 9 (Dublin, 1979), p. 260

Electronic Sources

Paul V. Walsh, *'The Irish Civil War 1922-1924: A Military Study of the Conventional phase 28 June-11 August 1922'*; Paper delivered to NYMAS at the CUNY graduate centre on 11 December 1998 available at http://libraryautomation.com/numas/irishcivilwar.html [11 November 2005]

THESES AND OTHER WORKS

Hall, Donal, 'World War I and national politics in Louth 1914-1920, in *Maynooth Series in Local History* (Dublin, 2005)

Murphy, Karl, 'General W.R.E. Murphy and the Irish Civil War' (M.A. thesis, NUI Maynooth, 1996)

Appendix

BRIEF CHRONOLOGY

1913-1924

13 January 1913	Ulster Volunteer Force formed in Belfast as a result of introduction of Third Home Rule Bill in April by Lloyd George.
25 November 1913	Inaugural meeting of the Irish Volunteers held in Dublin.
1 August 1914	Outbreak of First World War.
18 September 1914	Third Home Rule Bill placed on statute book - suspended until after the war.
20 September 1914	John Redmond's Irish Parliamentary Party urges the Irish Volunteers to enlist in the British Army. A split in the Volunteer movement occurs. The majority (170,000) follow Redmond and are renamed the 'National Volunteers', the rest (12,000) retain the 'Irish Volunteers' title.
24-29 April 1916	The Easter Rebellion.
11 November 1918	Armistice and end of First World War.
14 December 1918	General Election in Britain and Ireland. The Sinn Féin party wins majority of seats in Ireland and promises setting up of separate assembly to be known as *Dáil Eireann.*
21 January 1919	Dáil Éireann meets for the first time in the Mansion House Dublin as the Anglo-Irish War commences with an attack on Royal Irish Constabulary at Soloheadbeg, County Tipperary.
20 August 1919	Irish Volunteers swear allegiance to *Dail Éireann* and the Irish Republic.
2 January 1920	Recruitment begins in Britain for retired servicemen to serve in Ireland as police reinforcements.
25 February 1920	Government of Ireland Bill introduced in House of Commons providing for separate parliaments in North and South.

25 March 1920	New police reinforcements arrive in Ireland dressed in a mixture of dark green Royal Irish Constabulary (RIC) uniforms and British Army Khaki –and later nicknamed 'Black and Tans.'
27 July 1920	Recruitment begins in Britain for an Auxiliary division of the RIC made up of ex-British officers with combat experience.
25 October 1920	Terence MacSwiney, Lord Mayor of Cork, dies while on hunger strike in Brixton Prison.
21 November 1920 'Black	'Bloody Sunday.' 14 British intelligence agents assassinated in Dublin by Michael Collins' squad. In response the Auxiliaries shoot dead three Volunteers and a party of and Tans' open fire on a crowd of spectators and footballers at a Gaelic football match in Croke Park, killing 12.
28 November 1920	3rd Cork Brigade Flying Column attacks Auxiliary convoy in Kilmichael, County Cork, killing 17.
10 December 1920	Martial Law declared in counties Cork, Kerry, Limerick and Tipperary.
28 February 1921	Six Volunteer prisoners are executed in Victoria Barracks Cork. The IRA shoots six British soldiers in Cork City in response.
19 March 1921	3rd Cork Brigade Flying Column successfully ambush Crown forces convoy at Crossbarry, County Cork, inflicting many casualties.
11 July 1921	The Truce comes into effect and the Anglo-Irish War (Irish War of Independence) ends.
14 September 1921	Dáil Éireann selects five delegates to negotiate and conclude a settlement with the British Government.
6 December 1921	A Treaty between Great Britain and Ireland is finalised and signed. Southern Ireland is to be granted 'dominion' status and will be known as the Irish Free State and will have its own parliament, judiciary and defence force. All elected representatives are required to swear an oath of allegiance to the king. The six counties of Northern Ireland are to be a separate state with its own parliament.

7 January 1922   Dáil Éireann approves the Anglo-Irish Treaty by 64 votes to 57.

10 January 1922   Eamon de Valera is defeated in vote for presidency of the Dáil by 60 votes to 58 and leads his followers from the chamber.

14 January 1922   Pro-Treaty Dáil deputies approve resolutions to establish a Provisional Government, recognised by the British Government. Michael Collins appointed chairman; Richard Mulcahy is Minister of Defence and General Eoin O'Duffy becomes Chief of Staff of the new National Army.

16 January 1922   The Lord-Lieutenant, Edward Talbot Fitzallen, formally hands over power to Michael Collins at a ceremony in Dublin Castle. From this point British troops prepare to leave Ireland and the RIC begin preparations for disbandment. The IRA of the War of Independence (Irish Army) divides along Pro-Treaty and Anti-Treaty lines and these forces race to occupy vacated barracks throughout the country.

31 January 1922   The National Army (Pro –Treaty) takes over Beggar's Bush Barracks in Dublin and establishes its Head Quarters there.

1 April 1922   Churchill and Collins sign transfer of power from UK to *Saorstát Éireann* (Irish Free State).

9 April 1922   Anti-Treaty delegates attend an 'army' convention in Dublin. They elect their own 'army executive' with Liam Lynch as Chief of Staff.

13 April 1922   Anti-Treaty forces occupy the Four Courts in Dublin.

1 May 1922   Senior National pro-Treaty and anti- Treaty officers sign a document aimed at unification of the army.

16 June 1922   General Election held in Irish Free State with majority of those elected in favour of Anglo-Irish Treaty.

22 June 1922   IRA assassinates Sir Henry Wilson, military advisor to the government of Northern Ireland, in London. The British government demands action is taken by Free State authorities against dissident forces.

28 June 1922   The opening shots of the Irish Civil War are fired when Free State forces commence shelling of anti-Treaty forces occupying Four Courts in Dublin.

Ulster Solemn League and Covenant

Being convinced in our consciences that Home Rule would be disastrous to the material well-being of Ulster as well as the whole of Ireland, subversive of our civil and religious freedom, destructive of our citizenship and perilous to the unity of the Empire, we, whose names are under-written, men of Ulster, loyal subjects of His Gracious Majesty King George V., humbly relying on the God whom our fathers in days of stress and trial confidently trusted, do hereby pledge ourselves in solemn Covenant throughout this our time of threatened calamity to stand by one another in defending for ourselves and our children our cherished possession of equal citizenship in the United Kingdom and in using all means which may be found necessary to defeat the present conspiracy to set up a Home Rule Parliament in Ireland. And in the event of such a Parliament being forced upon us we further solemnly and mutually pledge ourselves to refuse to recognise its authority. In sure confidence that God will defend the right we hereto subscribe our names.

1916 Proclamation

IRISHMEN AND IRISHWOMEN: In the name of God and of the dead generations from which she receives her old tradition of nationhood, Ireland, through us, summons her children to her flag and strikes for her freedom.

Having organised and trained her manhood through her secret revolutionary organisation, the Irish Republican Brotherhood, and through her open military organisations, the Irish Volunteers and the Irish Citizen Army, having patiently perfected her discipline, having resolutely waited for the right moment to reveal itself, she now seizes that moment, and supported by her exiled children in America and by gallant allies in Europe, but relying in the first on her own strength, she strikes in full confidence of victory.

We declare the right of the people of Ireland to the ownership of Ireland and to the unfettered control of Irish destinies, to be sovereign and indefeasible. The long usurpation of that right by a foreign people and government has not extinguished the right, nor can it ever be extinguished except by the destruction of the Irish people. In every generation the Irish people have asserted their right to national freedom and sovereignty; six times during the past three hundred years they have asserted it in arms. Standing on that fundamental right and again asserting it in arms in the face of the world, we hereby proclaim the Irish Republic as a Sovereign Independent State, and we pledge our lives and the lives of our comrades in arms to the cause of its freedom, of its welfare, and of its exaltation among the nations.

The Irish Republic is entitled to, and herby claims, the allegiance of every Irishman and Irishwoman. The Republic guarantees religious and civil liberty, equal rights and equal opportunities to all its citizens, and declares its resolve to pursue the happiness and prosperity of the whole nation and of all its parts, cherishing all of the children of the nation equally, and oblivious of the differences carefully fostered by an alien Government, which have divided a minority from the majority in the past.

Until our arms have brought the opportune moment for the establishment of a permanent National Government, representative of the whole people of Ireland and elected by the suffrages of all her men and women, the Provisional Government, hereby constituted, will administer the civil and military affairs of the Republic in trust for the people.

We place the cause of the Irish Republic under the protection of the Most High God, Whose blessing we invoke upon our arms, and we pray that no one who serves that cause will dishonour it by cowardice, inhumanity, or rapine. In this supreme hour the Irish nation must, by its valour and discipline, and by the readiness of its children to sacrifice themselves for the common good, prove itself worthy of the august destiny to which it is called.

Signed on behalf of the Provisional Government:

> THOMAS J. CLARKE,
> SEAN Mac DIARMADA, THOMAS MacDONAGH,
> P.H. PEARSE, EAMONN CEANNT,
> JAMES CONNOLLY, JOSEPH PLUNKETT

The Anglo-Irish Treaty 1921

1. Ireland shall have the same constitutional status in the Community of Nations known as the British Empire as the Dominion of Canada, the Commonwealth of Australia, the Dominion of New Zealand and the Union of South Africa, with a Parliament having powers to make laws for the peace, order and good government of Ireland and an Executive responsible to that Parliament, and shall be styled and known as the Irish Free State.

2. Subject to the provisions hereinafter set out the position of the Irish Free State in relation to the Imperial Parliament and Government and otherwise shall be that of the Dominion of Canada, and the law practice and constitutional usage governing the relationship of the Crown or the representative of the Crown and of the Imperial Parliament to the Dominion of Canada shall govern their relationship to the Irish Free State.

3. The representative of the Crown in Ireland shall be appointed in like manner as   the Governor-General of Canada and in accordance with the practice observed in the making of such appointments.

4. The oath to be taken by Members of the Parliament of the Irish Free State shall be in the following form:

I ….. do solemnly swear true faith and allegiance to the Constitution of the Irish Free State as by law established and that I will be faithful to H.M. King George V, his heirs and successors by law, in virtue of the common citizenship of Ireland with Great Britain and her adherence to and membership of the group of nations forming the British Commonwealth of Nations.

5. The Irish Free State shall assume liability for the service of the Public Debt of the United Kingdom as existing at the date hereof and towards the payment of war pensions as existing at that date in such proportion as may be fair and equitable, having regard to any just claims on the part of Ireland by way of set-off or counter-claim, the amount of such sums being determined in default of agreement by the arbitration of one or more independent persons being citizens of the British Empire.

"I do solemnly swear true faith and allegiance to the Constitution of the Irish Free State."

6. Until an arrangement has been made between the British and Irish Governments whereby the Irish Free State undertakes her own coastal defence, the defence by sea of Great Britain and Ireland shall be undertaken by His Majesty's Imperial Forces. But this shall not prevent the construction or maintenance by the Government of the Irish Free State of such vessels as are necessary for the protection of the Revenue or the Fisheries.

The foregoing provisions of this Article shall be reviewed at a Conference of Representatives of the British and Irish Governments to be held at the expiration of five years from the date hereof with a view to a share in her own coastal defence.

7. The Government of the Irish Free State shall afford to His Majesty's Imperial Forces:

   (a) In time of peace such harbour and other facilities as are indicated in the Annex hereto, or such other facilities as may from time to time be agreed between the British Government and the Government of the Irish Free State; and

183

(b) In time of war or of strained relations with a Foreign Power such harbour and other facilities as the British Government may require for the purposes of such defence as aforesaid.

8. With a view to securing the observance of the principle of international limitation of armaments, if the Government of the Irish Free State establishes and maintains a military defence force, the establishments thereof shall not exceed in size such proportion of the military establishments maintained in Great Britain as that which the population of Ireland bears to the population of Great Britain.

9. The ports of Great Britain and the Irish Free State shall be freely open to the ships of the other country on payment of the customary port and other dues.

10. The Government of the Irish Free State agrees to pay fair compensation on terms not less favourable than those accorded by the Act of 1920 to judges, officials, members of Police Forces and other Public Servants who are discharged by it or who retire in consequence of the change of Government effected in pursuance hereof.

[It is] provided that this agreement shall not apply to members of the Auxiliary Police Force or to persons recruited in Great Britain for the Royal Irish Constabulary during the two years next preceding the date hereof. The British Government will assume responsibility for such compensation or pensions as may be payable to any of these excepted persons.

11. Until the expiration of one month from the passing of the Act of Parliament for the ratification of this instrument, the powers of the Parliament and the Government of the Irish Free State shall not be exercisable as respects Northern Ireland and the provisions of the Government of Ireland Act, 1920, shall so far as they relate to Northern Ireland remain of full force and effect, and no election shall be held for the return of members to serve in the Parliament of the Irish Free State for constituencies in Northern Ireland, unless a resolution is passed by both Houses of the Parliament of Northern Ireland in favour of the holding of such election before the end of the said month.

'The powers of the Parliament and Government of the Irish Free State shall no longer extend to Northern Ireland.'

12. If before the expiration of the said month, an address is presented to His Majesty by both Houses of the Parliament of Northern Ireland to that effect, the powers of the Parliament and Government of the Irish Free State shall no longer extend to Northern Ireland, and the provisions of the Government of Ireland Act, 1920 (including those relating to the Council of Ireland) shall, so far as they relate to Northern Ireland, continue to be of full force and effect, and this instrument shall have effect subject to the necessary modifications.

Provided that if such an address is so presented a Commission consisting of three Persons, one to be appointed by the Government of the Irish Free State, one to be appointed by the Government of Northern Ireland and one who shall be Chairman to be appointed by the British Government shall determine in accordance with the wishes of the inhabitants, so far as may be compatible with economic and geographic conditions, the boundaries between Northern Ireland and the rest of Ireland, and for the purposes of the Government of Ireland Act, 1920, and of this instrument, the boundary of Northern Ireland shall be such as may be determined by such Commission.

13. For the purpose of the last foregoing article, the powers of the Parliament of Southern Ireland under the Government of Ireland Act, 1920, to elect members of the Council of Ireland shall after the Parliament of the Irish Free State is constituted be exercised by that Parliament.

14. After the expiration of the said month, if no such address as is mentioned in Article 12 hereof is presented, the Parliament and Government of Northern Ireland shall continue to exercise as respects Northern Ireland the powers conferred on them by the Government of Ireland Act, 1920, but the Parliament and Government of the Irish Free State shall in Northern Ireland have in relation to matters in respect of which the Parliament of Northern Ireland has not power to make laws under that Act (including matters which under the said Act are within the jurisdiction of the Council of Ireland) the same powers as in the rest of Ireland, subject to such other provisions as may be agreed in manner hereinafter appearing.

15. At any time after the date hereof the Government of Northern Ireland and the provisional Government of Southern Ireland hereinafter constituted may meet for the purpose of discussing the provisions subject to which the last foregoing article is to operate in the event of no such address as is therein mentioned being presented and those provisions may include:

    (a) Safeguards with regard to patronage in Northern Ireland:

    (b) Safeguards with regard to the collection of revenue in Northern Ireland:

    (c) Safeguards with regard to import and export duties affecting the trade or industry of Northern Ireland:

(**d**) Safeguards for minorities in Northern Ireland:

(**e**) The settlement of the financial relations between Northern Ireland and the Irish Free State:

(**f**) The establishment and powers of a local militia in Northern Ireland and the relation of the Defence Forces of the Irish Free State and of Northern Ireland respectively:

and if at any such meeting provisions are agreed to, the same shall have effect as if they were included amongst the provisions subject to which the Powers of the Parliament and Government of the Irish Free State are to be exercisable in Northern Ireland under Article 14 hereof.

'Neither the Parliament of the Irish Free State nor the Parliament of Northern Ireland shall make any law so as . . . to . . . restrict the free exercise . . . of religious belief.'

16. Neither the Parliament of the Irish Free State nor the Parliament of Northern Ireland shall make any law so as either directly or indirectly to endow any religion or prohibit or restrict the free exercise thereof or give any preference or impose any disability on account of religious belief or religious status or affect prejudicially the right of any child to attend a school receiving public money without attending religious instruction at the school or make any discrimination as respects state aid between schools under the management of different religious denominations or divert from any religious denomination or any educational institution any of its property except for public utility purposes and on payment of compensation.

17. By way of provisional arrangement for the administration of Southern Ireland during the interval which must elapse between the date hereof and the constitution of a Parliament and Government of the Irish Free State in accordance therewith, steps shall be taken forthwith for summoning a meeting of members of Parliament elected for constituencies in Southern Ireland since the passing of the Government of Ireland Act, 1920, and for constituting a provisional Government, and the British Government shall take the steps necessary to transfer to such provisional Government the powers and machinery requisite for the discharge of its duties, provided that every member of such provisional Government shall have signified in writing his or her acceptance of this instrument. But this arrangement shall not continue in force beyond the expiration of twelve months from the date hereof.

18. This instrument shall be submitted forthwith by His Majesty's Government for the approval of Parliament and by the Irish signatories to a meeting summoned for the purpose of the members elected to sit in the House of Commons of Southern Ireland, and if approved shall be ratified by the necessary legislation.

On behalf of the Irish Delegation.	On behalf of the British Delegation.
Signed	*Signed*
ART Ó GRÍOBHTHA.	D. LLOYD GEORGE.
MICHEAL Ó COILÉAIN.	AUSTEN CHAMBERLAIN.
RIOBÁRD BARTÚN.	BIRKENHEAD.
EUDHMONN S. Ó DÚGÁIN.	WINSTON S. CHURCHILL.
SEÓRSA GHABHÁIN UÍ DHUBHTHAIGH.	L. WORTHINGTON-EVANS.
	HAMAR GREENWOOD.
	GORDON HEWART.

December 6th, 1921